ST. BRIDES BAY

Whitland

NARBERTH

Amroth

CALDY I.

HAVERFORDWEST

PEMBROKE

St. Govan's Head

Johnston

MILFORD HAVEN

Nolton

Linney Head

Talbenny

St. Ann's Head

SKOMER I.

SKOKHOLM I.

D1610546

DISPOSED OF
BY LIBRARY
HOUSE OF LORDS

10 miles

10 kilometres

0

0

The Pembrokeshire Coast Path

John H. Barrett

Long-Distance Footpath Guide No 3

London Her Majesty's Stationery Office 1974
Published for the Countryside Commission

The maps in this guide are extracts from
Ordnance Survey maps 1:25,000 or about
2½ Inches to 1 Mile and have been
prepared from production material
supplied by Ordnance Survey. Sheets
SN03, 04, 10, 14; SM70, 72, 80, 81, 82, 83,
90; SR99; SS09, 19; 12/93.

Drawings by Ronald Maddox
Nature drawings by Harry Titcombe

The views expressed are those of the
author and not necessarily of the
Countryside Commission.

Government Bookshops
49 High Holborn, London WC1V 6HB
13A Castle Street, Edinburgh EH2 3AR
41 The Hayes, Cardiff CF1 1JW
Brazennose Street, Manchester M60 8AS
Southey House, Wine Street, Bristol BS1 2BQ
258 Broad Street, Birmingham B1 2HE
80 Chichester Street, Belfast BT1 4JY
*Government publications are also
available through booksellers*

Prepared for the
Countryside Commission by the
Central Office of Information

The waymark sign is
used in plaque or stencil
form by the Countryside
Commission on long-
distance footpaths

Printed in England for Her Majesty's
Stationery Office by W. S. Cowell Ltd.,
Ipswich, Suffolk

iv Dd 503659 K80   ISBN 0 11 700336 0

Maps

Foreword

I hope this guide adds to the pleasure of those who walk along our path by telling them some of the things they might not otherwise have known. I have enjoyed writing it. I hope too that some will be persuaded that the splendours of spring and autumn, and even of midwinter, surpass those of high summer.

My thanks are due—and these are not just formal thanks—above all to my wife. On so many days during the field work she has dropped me at the starting point, met me at lunch-time and again at the end of the stint and so saved me having to make my way back to the car at the starting point. Both of us discovered parts of the coast we did not know before.

Throughout all the years the making of the path has been directed by Paul Blick, at that time the only paid Warden in the national park. Nobody used initiative and diplomacy as he did; nobody received so many brickbats and ignorant rudery. Had Paul Blick always kept to the usual channels our path would not have been walkable for another decade. Happily he continues to oversee it from his base in the County Council offices, Haverfordwest. He has helped me generously with his knowledge of details.

Then my colleague, Ieuan Griffiths, has told me many useful things. He and Dillwyn Miles have helped me with their native Welsh. The Commandants of the Castlemartin R.A.C. range and the R.A. School of Artillery at Manorbier allowed me access along their coasts. County Council officers in the Planning and Surveyor's Departments have answered many questions for me.

I am truly grateful to all these people.

John H. Barrett

A path for all

The report proposing that a Pembrokeshire Coast path should be established was approved on 3 July 1953, a year after designation of the Pembrokeshire Coast as the fifth national park had been confirmed. This path was planned to follow the 168 miles from the Carmarthenshire frontier, round the national park coastline of Pembrokeshire and up to the Cardiganshire boundary.

The great majority of the landowners approached in Pembrokeshire were reasonable and even generous in their response to the path and quickly signed footpath dedications where new rights-of-way were required. Eventually there remained only a hard core of objectors who used every legal and administrative device to postpone the day on which strangers might walk the rough edge of the cliffs round their land—in most cases a rough edge so overgrown with gorse and blackthorn that the owner had no possible alternative use for it. One estate in the south even forbade access to the

Little Haven.

officials who wished to map out a tentative route so that a basis for negotiation might exist. Such opposition demanded diligence and patience from the staff of local authorities.

When in due course the line was legally established, the problems of making a passable path arose. This is easy to talk about in the abstract, on the ground it is quite another thing. Thickets of gorse and bramble, steep screes, boggy bottoms, long lengths remote from even a small lane were only some of the problems which confronted an entirely inadequate manpower. In some stretches a mini-bulldozer was used and those who walk the path will find it incredible that a piece of machinery could have been manoeuvred over such terrain. Field banks have been straddled by oak stiles and heavy baulks shifted to bridge streams.

On the windward cliffs where the bulldozer had only heather and low gorse to contend with, the scars of its passing were, to begin with, unpleasantly conspicuous. Those who launch into tirades about desecrating the coast refuse to believe that if the path had not been cut mechanically it would not have been established at all.

The line of the path is as near to the cliff edge as is practicable. Finding the way is not the kind of problem it can be on the great upland stretches of the Pennine Way, for instance. The whole length is through a landscape of details, which can be easily read on the 2½-in. O.S. maps. The field banks, streams, coastal features and individual buildings will give the walker a fix to within a few yards. It is impossible to be lost. Oak Coastal Path finger-posts are a help where provided, but nothing like all the path is marked in this or any other way.

Over some stretches the path is forced back from the cliff. The Castlemartin tank range prevents access to some five miles round Linney Head. With any luck the Royal Artillery may leave Manorbier and we will then have access again to Skrinkle Haven and Old Castle Head. While the oil companies made provision for the path on the seaward side of their perimeters, the Central Electricity Generating Board persuaded the authorities that this could not be done at the Pembroke power station. Between the power station and Hobb's Point, and between Waterwynch and Tenby, at Druidston and in one or two other places, short detours from the cliff are forced by the nature of the ground or by the justifiable claim to privacy from owners of property built long before the path was thought of. While making these detours the walker is almost never out of sight of the sea.

The path was officially opened on 16 May 1970 by Mr. Wynford Vaughan-Thomas, President of the Council for the Protection of Rural Wales. In his speech he echoed the thought that we now have 168 miles of the most beautiful coast in Britain open for anybody to enjoy. No path, he said, is as easy to maintain as a well used one. If only a few people use this path, then continuing objections to spending money on its maintenance will be increasingly easy to press on the authorities. Access along these lengths of incomparable coast will dwindle away if not enough people insist that it be maintained as the Government intended it should be when it was approved in 1953.

Tenby.

The shaping of the coastline

Pembrokeshire is nothing if not an ancient landscape. The county is based upon an unbroken series of rocks piled up on the igneous/volcanic Pre-Cambrian base which cooled, when at last the earth began to be solid, some 3,000 million years ago. As soon as evaporation led to the first fall of rain, these original thicknesses were eroded and washed down into the sea. The systems of sedimentary rocks began to accumulate; along the Pembrokeshire coast they pass upwards through the Cambrian, Ordovician, Silurian, Old Red Sandstone and Carboniferous. Their relative ages and thicknesses are summarised opposite and their general arrangement in the county is shown in the map at the beginning of the guide. Although rocks younger than the Carboniferous were probably laid down in Pembrokeshire, they have all been eroded off.

The history of the earth's surface includes periods of violent disturbance in the crust, spreading outward from a centre as waves progress across a pond when a stone is thrown into it. The waves of pressure buckle the rocks into up-folds and down-folds, thicknesses may crack and the rock on one side of the crack move in relation to that on the other side. Later waves of pressure may thrust up one mass to override another, the folds may be steepened and crack along their axies, as a sheet of cardboard cracks and buckles if bent too much.

After such a disturbance very long periods of quiet produce further systems of sedimentary rocks (sandstones, limestones, conglomerates, shales), to be followed by a second mountain-building disturbance, during which these newer rocks are folded and faulted. In consequence, the contortions previously imposed on the older systems are modified and perhaps exaggerated.

4   From time to time throughout the whole geological

Age in millions of years	Period or System	Formation	Thickness
		Except for glacial materials, peat and blown sand, all the rocks deposited during the last 250 million years have been eroded away again and have left no trace behind them.	
250	——— ARMORICAN EARTH MOVEMENTS ———		
	Carboniferous	Coal Measures	6000 ft. at least
		Millstone Grit	900 ft.
		Carboniferous Limestone	1500 ft. at least
350			
	Old Red Sandstone	Upper	500–1000 ft.
		Lower	2000–3000 ft.
400	———CALEDONIAN EARTH MOVEMENTS ———		
	Silurian	Upper or Ludlow	900–2000 ft.
		Middle or Wenlock	400–500 ft.
		Lower or Llandovery	500–800 ft.
440			
	Ordovician	Bala	1200 ft.
		Llandilo	1000 ft.
		Llanvirn	1000 ft.
		Arenig	1500–3000 ft.
500			
	Cambrian	Upper	2000 ft.
		Middle	1900 ft. at least
		Lower	1500 ft.
600	———CHARNIAN EARTH MOVEMENTS———		
	Pre-Cambrian	Intrusive granites, etc.	
		Extrusive lavas, ashes, etc.	
3000			

The geological column in Pembrokeshire.

sequence, minor volcanic disturbances may squeeze up molten magma into the covering of sedimentary rocks. This intrusive heat, as with the heat from folding and faulting, may bake the layers into which it intrudes and so change their nature, e.g. the metamorphosis of sandstone into quartzite. Two of these earth-storms have affected Pembrokeshire. At the end of Silurian times the Caledonian movement imposed its SW–NE trend on the north of the county. All the long lines on the map and the axes of the dominant features of the topography of the north coast stem from this disturbance which had died away before the Old Red Sandstone and Carboniferous depositions began.

5

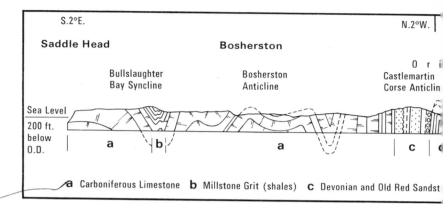

Section through the rocks of South Pembrokeshire (redrawn from section of Geological Survey 1-inch sheet 245 by permission of the Director, Institute of Geological Sciences).

The Old Red and Carboniferous rocks underlie the south of the county. The Armorican storm came at the end of Carboniferous times. It was centred in Brittany (Armorica) and its pressures from the south produced the WNW–ESE trend in south Pembrokeshire. The south was squeezed up against the relatively immovable north. The alignment of the northern rocks was modified in places and additional faulting redoubled the Caledonian complications. By contrast the south of the county is a relatively simple series of up-folds and down-folds. The individual layers of rock are tilted at all angles, even over the vertical. Indications of this "dip" are marked on the maps of the path by arrows pointing in the directions to which the beds dip, the number alongside noting the angle, which is always read down from the horizontal.

Sea-level is not fixed for all time. In the past the sea has been hundreds of feet lower, and many hundreds of feet higher, than it is now. The whole Pembrokeshire coastland is dominated by a level platform cut by the waves some seventeen million years ago at the beginning of the Pliocene period. In the south, almost all the variations caused by folding were planed off by the waves to give a flat-topped landscape—the famous 200-foot erosion surface. In the north the more ancient

6 volcanic and igneous rocks were so hard that the waves

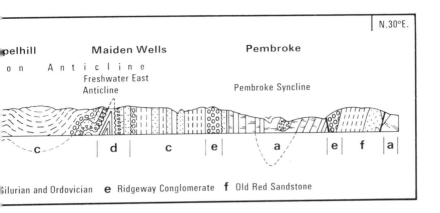

pelhill · Maiden Wells · Pembroke

on Anticline
Freshwater East
Anticline
Pembroke Syncline

Silurian and Ordovician · **e** Ridgeway Conglomerate · **f** Old Red Sandstone

had insufficient time to reduce them all to the uniform level. The "monadnocks" which stand up above the erosion surface are the surviving stacks and islands of those seas and are in just the same relation to the 200-foot surface as our stacks and islands to the present sea-level. But those who walk our coastal path will find it hard to believe that they traverse a flat surface. Each small stream runs at the bottom of a deep valley. By the end of the day the walker is more conscious of climbing steeply than making level progress.

When the sea fell off the 200-foot surface (or the land lifted up—same result), at once the rain came down, small streams began to run downhill into larger streams and into the rivers, and so on down to the sinking sea-level. This new drainage system exploited the weaknesses in the surface; breaks caused by Caledonian and Armorican faulting and folding presented an easy way down to the sea. Differential hardness in the rocks determined, as always, the shape of the drainage pattern. Since leaving the 200-foot surface the sea has never returned. So the streams and rivers have had time to incise their courses deeply. But the present flow of water down these valleys, no matter for how long it ran, could never have caused the erosion of rock which has taken place. We have to come forward to only yesterday, in geological time, that is, to find the necessary extra erosive force.

Some 15,000 years ago the ice was melting and releasing huge volumes of water to drain down these valleys, the line of which had been established long, 7 long before glacial times. So much water had been taken up into the ice that sea-level was then some 300 feet lower than now. Thus the melt-water ran down a much steeper slope than survives in the remaining stream profiles. The combination of volume and speed was sufficient to gouge out and widen courses. The dramatic valleys behind Solva, Lower Fishguard and Nevern are classical glacial overflow channels, but all the other streams too were then large enough to widen and deepen their valleys to the size they are today. Climbing up yet again to the 200-foot surface, the walker will reflect on the influence of water in shaping the landscape.

Indeed so much water ran into the sea that rising sea-levels drowned the lower courses of the drainage system. The pre-glacial course of the Cleddau is now the deep-water channel in the Haven. The oil companies' piers have to be long enough to reach out from the rocky shore across what was the flat flood-plain to this deep channel. Salt water reaches now right up to Haverfordwest; Porthclais and the Solva valleys were drowned, and so too the Ritec valley up to St. Florence and the streams that now run through the Bosherston lily ponds. In late medieval times a sandbar developed across the mouth of these last two and so impeded the flow of the tide that, in each case, the final separation of the valley from the sea was a simple man-built wall.

The ice that affected Pembrokeshire originated in the Hebrides, having flowed south across north-east Ireland before being joined by glaciers sliding down from the Lake District. The ice, when it reached Pembrokeshire, mainly lodged against our western and northern coasts, but in some places it flowed inland. At the melting stage all the gravel, stones and boulders that had been gathered into the mass as it shovelled its way south, fell through to the ground below. When the ice had almost gone, but while the ground was still frozen tundra (permafrost), some of these stones slid down from both sides into the valley bottoms.

These processes are clearly marked along the coastal path. Over long lengths, the cliff section is capped with glacial sand and gravel (boulder clay), up to ten feet thick or more in hollows, and mixed with large angular blocks (head) at the bottom of steeper valleys. Scattered along the edge of the cliffs are large and small boulders, rocks foreign to what is below. Some of these "erratics" have travelled all the way from the Hebrides, others from only a few miles across St. Bride's Bay. Their presence helps to determine the direction of ice movement. Indeed, so common are these glacial features along the coast that attention is drawn on the maps only to special cases.

Our coast is sinking into the sea again. About half an inch every hundred years may not sound dangerous but as a geologist measures time it will not be long before the sea is back on the 200-foot surface. Certainly day-by-day the tide is in contact with the foot of the cliffs; day-by-day the age-old processes of erosion and denudation continue to sharpen and renew the multiplicity of angles, headlands, stacks, islands, beaches and bays.

The walker along the cliff path is sometimes rather too far up to see the details of this fretting. He has to content himself with the sweep of the scene. A single principle underlies the complexity: soft material is eroded faster than hard. A thickness, like coal, may be soft because of its nature; rocks of any hardness may have been broken, and so softened, by folding, faulting or cracking (jointing). Whatever the cause, the soft thickness will be cut into by the waves faster than the harder on either side. The same principle, on a larger scale, leads to the development of St. Bride's Bay or Carmarthen Bay, where soft Coal Measures are worn back faster than the hard wings of those bays, as applies to any length of a few feet of cliff.

Often a weakness (softness) passes through a peninsula and is attacked by the waves on both sides. Two caves are gradually hollowed out and become so big that at last a fall of rock unites the two into an arch. The pillar supporting the arch has its own weaknesses which continue to be exploited by the waves. Gradually the base of the pillar is so reduced that the arch crashes down; what was a pillar is now a great stack. It is worn down and down to become at length no more than a residue of its former self. In the end all is brought down to the level of the wave-cut platform. This end-product of erosion stretches off-shore for an unknown distance; at low tide it appears as the floor of the bays all round the coast. Should the sea-level fall, that platform would appear as another flat surface directly comparable with 9 the 200-foot platform. The sequence of promontory, caves, arch, stack and residual stack is displayed nowhere more clearly than in the Carboniferous Limestone of the south coast.

A shingle bar is heaped across the back of many bays. The stones are thrown forward and upward by the waves, but, because so much of the water percolates down into the stones, they are not dragged back by the retreating waves. The outer face of the shingle is ridged, indicating heights of varying tides. The top of the bank is at the level to which stones are thrown during storms. The generic name for these bars is "storm-beach". The stream in the valley on the landward side may be deflected to run for a distance parallel with the beach and then it normally percolates through the barrier; but after heavy rains it may burst out through any gap it makes. The lowest lengths of the valley floor inland are boggy.

Sand-dunes accumulate across the width of some valleys, particularly those which face the prevailing south and south-west winds, where gently shelving sandy shores are exposed at low tide. Quick drying by sun and wind leaves the surface sand blowing off to landward. The sand may move inland and engulf good farmland. Normally it is fixed by the introduction of marram grass which continues to flourish as long as fresh sand is being added. The turf which develops in the botanical succession stabilises the dunes but is thin and tender. Too many feet, burrowing rabbits, let alone the tyres of cars, burst through to produce a "blow-out" which gales rapidly enlarge and the whole dune system may be in movement inland again. The walker round Pembrokeshire will find evidence enough that much stricter lines of access will have to be established at Newport, Whitesand and Freshwater West and East if our sand-dune systems are not soon to be destroyed.

The path repeatedly crosses these various types of shore, sometimes on the leeward side of the county, and more often up to windward. Exposure and shelter, the forceful buffeting of the wind, the deposition of salt whipped up from the crests of winter's waves, sunshine or shadow at midday—all these variables are expressed not only in the physical nature of lengths of shore, but
also in the plants and animals that live along them.

Flowers of the coast

By far the greatest part of the Pembrokeshire coast is rocky; some of the cliffs are vertical, some less abruptly sloping. Across the back of many of the smaller bays are graded banks of stones, on some of which shingle bank vegetation flourishes. Behind some of these banks salt-marsh plants may colonise the mud and indicate the gradation to freshwater. Where the shingle bank excludes the sea, the valley bottom may be a bog. In the big bays in the south and in the estuaries at Newport and Poppit in the north, sand-dunes have accumulated and are stabilised by that complex of beautiful plants based on the pioneer work of marram grass. The walker finds himself crossing yet another assemblage of plants when he strides across the many small streams which, particularly in the north, fall down precipitous little waterfalls into the sea.

This variety of habitat is further refined by the twists in the line of the coast, presenting some lengths to the full fury of winter gales and soaking by salt spray carried up from the waves. Gales (Force 8 and upwards) are so common that the 31·5 days of gale recorded in an average year at St. Ann's Head are not notably fewer than the 38·8 days of calm. Gusts of up to 90 m.p.h. are not unusual and these are the occasions that impose the pattern of vegetation on the cliffs. The drier the wind and the greater the speed, the greater the rate of cooling by evaporation, to the point that spring gales may "burn" back the tender shoots of trees which then appear to lean to leeward.

Some lengths of coast are so tucked round corners as to be almost entirely sheltered from this buffeting. Both exposed and sheltered lengths may be in full sunshine or deep shadow at midday; they may be on either steep or gentle slopes, with soil derived from acid rocks or 11 basic or from glacial material or a mixture. All these variables will occur in any combination to give a refinement of detail that helps to explain the splendour of the coastal flowers in Pembrokeshire.

The scrub oaks south of Saundersfoot and overhanging Goultrop Roads may represent a remnant of what the wooded areas once were. Nowadays Sycamore is more likely to dominate these sheltered slopes unless modern forestry has introduced Pine, Larch or Spruce. The floor of the woods is deeply covered in Male, Soft Shield and Polypody ferns and often, too, with the thick shiny dark green Hart's-tongue or the yellower long lance leaves of Hairy Woodrush. Primroses, Wood Anemones, Bluebells and Red Campion provide much of the colour. Round the edges of the wood, where a broken tree canopy allows in enough light, brambles build an impenetrable thicket.

As the wind pressure increases, the trees become misshapen by die-back of the windward buds. Elder and Blackthorn nurse the last surviving trees on the windward edge and themselves tail off into a thicket of brambles in which Gorse and Bracken become commoner as the last tree finally disappears. Out of the trees, and yet still sheltered from the full fury of the gales, stands of Foxglove, with fields of Bluebells, flourish marvellously. Various other woodland plants persist; Wood-sage, Wood-sorrel, Groundsel and the Slender False Broom grass, all flourish too because the air along the windward cliffs is as damp as in the bottom of the woods inland.

Where they would be exposed to the full blast of the gale, the Elder and Bracken no longer survive and the Blackthorn is layered downwind close to the shape of the land. Heather survives here and sweeps of Bluebells.

Those who have never seen our windward cliffs in late May and June will judge a description of them to be exaggerated. Take almost any patch for exhibition at the Chelsea Flower Show and the rock garden medal would be yours!

By the end of March the Scurvy-grass whitens in patches, Celandines shine in sunny hollows and the Primroses open, with bunches of Violets and the brilliance of the first Dandelions. Throughout April the colours multiply. The elusive blue of Vernal Squill spreads over the fescue turf: among tumbled stones the Sea Campion begins to open white bells and the Gorse flowers weigh down the air with scent. Sea-pinks begin to dominate the very exposed turf, with spikes of purple Sea Milkwort thrusting between. The rock outcrops are covered in patterns of grey, brown and vivid orange lichens and, wherever nutrients can collect in some tiny crack, English Stone-crop and Spurrey will survive. Drifts of Ox-eye Daisies reach down the cliffs and, in extreme exposure, unashamedly flaring yellow Prostrate Broom outshines all others. Lady's Fingers delicately elaborate this yellow theme.

By mid-May, Bluebells haze long lines of cliffs, and Red Campion and Foxgloves add contrasting tones. The redshot canary-yellow of Bird's-foot Trefoil begins to appear and the round blue-purple heads of Sheep's-bit. On slopes towards the full blast of the gales and the salt spray, tussocks of Thrift range from palest pink to deep crimson. The short Red Fescue turf of the path is starred with Sea Storksbill and Hart's-horn Plantain and small clovers add their details. By the first of June all the promise of the spring has been redeemed. High summer needs a different covering.

In July the Wild Carrot thrusts lacy leaves and flat pink-white heads of flower so attractive to the Soldier Beetles. Hawkbits and Hawkweeds stand stiffly lemon and yellow; the Silverweed and Tormentil add large and small stars to the turf. In some hollows are complicated blues of Viper's-bugloss. Minute Pearlworts, Sea Mayweeds, the pink of Centaury, yellow and white Lady's and Heath Bedstraws, purple Hardheads and banks of Thyme and Heather, in August on the Pembrokeshire cliffs, are so beautifully matched with the full duck-egg-yolk yellow of the Welsh Gorse.

This near-random dotting through the list of shapes and colours and seasons can only hint at the total splendour of flowers, blue sea and trailing cloud shadows. If the path was only along exposed cliff tops the botanist would have constant delight; but his other opportunities are many.

The sand-dune environment is occupied by quite a different community of plants. Marram grass first stabilises the sand and continues to flourish as long as fresh sand is being added; but at the seaward foot of the dunes it is Sea Rocket, Sea Couchgrass, Orache and Sea-beet that first use the nourishment from the rotting tideline. Once tufts of Marram provide enough shelter, Ragwort, thistles and Sand Sedge can survive, and Silverweed, spurges and Creeping Buttercup thicken up the turf and add yellows to the dominant grey-greens.

From that stage on, the dune turf becomes an enchanting mosaic of lovely plants: Scarlet Pimpernel, Dog Violets, Heath Milkwort, Rest Harrow, Speedwells, Sticky Chickweeds and Thyme-leaved Sandwort, and winding in among them the watered purple trumpets of Sea Bindweed. Mosses and lichens close up this community and conserve more moisture.

The turf that looks and feels so firm to a man's foot is really thin and fragile. Break through to the sand below and the next gale will expand the damage as sand blows out to leeward, smothering the coastal farmer's fields and entirely destroying the long years of capture which started when the Marram spread into the sand originally. So it is that the walker may find his way rather closely defined, perhaps by a sleepered trackway, and cars may be forbidden altogether from this fragile habitat.

Large shingle banks like the Chesil Beach or the mouth of the Alde in Suffolk are desolate, but those in Pembrokeshire are all small, many of them occupying the base of bays, and so much visited in summer that the particular vegetation that used to clothe their tops has now been destroyed by the feet of holiday-makers. Yet there are lengths where Sea Couchgrass and species of Orache and Sea-beet invade the spring-tide level, while, just above, the Woody Nightshade and the special variety of Curled Dock go up to the top of the bank where the glaucous crinkled leaves of the Horned Poppy are surmounted by the pale watery yellow flower which later develops the long bent seed-pod from which the plant's name derives. This graceful flower is so obvious and so scarce that the walker should take particular trouble to leave it alone.

Some of these shingle banks have salt-marshes behind them. These marshes are completely covered by high spring tides and not reached at all by the lowest neap high water. In hot weather, during the neaps, the water may evaporate and leave crystalline salt glistening on the mud; but during periods of incessant rain every trace of salt may be washed out. Only a few species of flowering plant can survive in this range of salinity. Lower down the Glasswort and Sea-blite colonise the mud; thick mattresses of Sea Purslane border the drainage channels and slow up the water movement so that the suspended grains of silt fall to the ground and steadily build up the level of the marsh. The sward at the top of the salt-marsh is covered by pink Thrift in May and then changes to all the subtle shades of Sea Lavender in August. The stiff little Sea Milkwort is tucked into the turf round the edge of the marsh. Rather like the Yellow-hammer, if Sea Milkwort were rare it would be famous for its beauty.

The plants of all the coast are beautiful. In themselves they are a sufficient reason for walking the path. In the first week of January, in all but the coldest years, more than fifty species would be in flower. During spring and summer their abundance is a glory. The long-distance path passes through good examples of all the coastal habitats famous for their flowers.

Nesting, migrant and winter birds

The great variety of habitat round the Pembrokeshire coast is inevitably mirrored in the long list of birds that occur there. During a year a hundred and fifty species or more could be seen from the path as it makes its way through woods and thickets, along sheltered estuaries and exposed Atlantic cliffs. The population in the middle of winter is at least as large as in midsummer, because then so many northern birds have moved down to enjoy our mild weather. When Scotland and the north of England are gripped by ice and snow, the coast of Pembrokeshire is the refuge for untold numbers of Redwings, Fieldfares, Starlings, Peewits, Snipe, Woodcock, Water-rails, finches of various kinds, larks, pipits, many ducks, pigeons, buntings and grebes. I am sure that eighty-five, and possibly one hundred, species could be seen from the path during the first week of January.

In the middle of summer, the breathless business of feeding young combines with all the cover in trees and bushes to produce an impression of comparative emptiness. But, of course, the woods are then full of tits and warblers, the thickets shelter Hedge-sparrows, Robins, Yellow-hammers, Chaffinches, Bullfinches and Whitethroats. As the line of the cliff turns to face the wind, Skylarks and Meadow-pipits dominate the farmland, with some Starlings and Rooks. Along the cliff, Jackdaws are increasingly conspicuous and Rock-pipits test the precision of the walker's power of observation. The Stonechat flicks his tail from the tiptop of a gorsebush and, on ground too rough for the plough, the white rump of a Wheatear disappears behind a rock.

All along these taller cliffs, small groups of Herring

Gulls may be nesting and parties of Fulmars secrete their nests almost always where they cannot be reached. The Fulmar steadily becomes more common; in 1949, Pembrokeshire's first egg was laid, on Skomer; since then something like twenty-five small colonies have become established.

The Choughs survive. Until about 1950 their numbers were declining and we feared a similar fate to those that used to live in Cornwall. But in recent years the number of breeding pairs has increased a little and is now up to fifty, spread fairly evenly all round the coast. On any day the walker may expect to see them.

Buzzards nest at wide intervals along these cliffs, their numbers increasing again after the disaster of myxomatosis. Ravens are common enough to be commonplace, building large nests of sticks locked on to inaccessible ledges half-way up the cliff. The Kestrels too nest all round the coast. In the days before chlorinated hydrocarbons one would have seen a Peregrine almost any day along the cliff. Then they disappeared. Now, slowly, slowly, they are coming back. Two eyries have recently been occupied, the locations having to be closely guarded because of the growing craze for falconry which, stimulated unduly by that lovely film "Kes", encourages far too many ruthless operators to steal the young.

Peregrines largely feed on pigeons. All round the coast are parties of multi-coloured pigeons, some grey, others white or brown with all the patchwork of variation that betokens a hybrid swarm. Some have totally resumed the blue-grey of true Rock Pigeons, with a double dark wing bar and creamy rump. All "fancy" pigeons are derived from Rock Pigeons; when they escape from loft or farmyard to breed without selection, in a few generations their progeny reverts to the plumage of the original wild stock. This process is well illustrated in these coastal parties. Meanwhile they are meat for the Peregrines.

Although their habitats overlap, Cormorants are usually in estuaries and sheltered water, while Shags are along the full exposure of the Atlantic cliffs. Few of either species breed along the mainland but both are to be found on the islands, the Shag in the shelter of jumbled rocks or under a little overhang, while the 17

Cormorant nests among the vegetation of St. Margaret's or the Mew Stone. All the year round they fish by diving from the sea's surface, the Cormorant tucking his head down before sliding below, while the Shag gives a little jump that momentarily carries it clear of the surface before plopping under.

A little off shore the Gannet also dives. This shining white sea-bird, with black tips to wings that stretch six feet across, plunges from a hundred feet or more after Mackerel or Herring in season and Pollack when nothing better is about. The wings, half-closed, flick corrections of line until the moment of entry. During the descent air sacs in its neck are inflated to absorb the impact and save a broken neck. The colony of 15,000 pairs on Grassholm steadily gets larger and has long since been the biggest in England and Wales.

For many sea-birds the islands have an attraction which no human eye can measure. Razorbills (which grace the national park badge), Guillemots, Puffins, the nocturnal Shearwaters and Storm Petrels, the Kittiwakes, Greater and Lesser Black-backed Gulls, all congregate on these off-shore islands in breeding colonies that count up into thousands of pairs. From the long-distance path the walker will see no more than little groups on a few isolated stacks, or black and white dots rather far off, either on the sea or flying with fast flickering wings low over the swell. Just as summer dark overtakes the last remnant of daylight, rafts of Shearwaters may drift past the large headlands, thin black wings stiffly careening in an elegance of curve not surpassed by wood pigeon in the ecstasy of display.

Almost all round the coast the Oyster-catcher (they do *not* catch oysters) nests among the rocks low down. Handsome in black and white, with orange legs and beak, they pipe, in early summer, those floods of notes that are taken up in chorus. Curlew are back inland wherever the ground is wet.

Those who hope to see waders will wait until the autumn migration brings them down our coast from the north. The Common Sandpiper is back by 21 July, with the first young Redshank of the year. As August passes into September the Whimbrel, plovers, Dunlin, godwits and Turnstone are common along the estuaries of Cleddau, Gann and Nevern. The terns stream south in

October. At the same time the main weight of migration passing down the western coasts of Europe pauses in Pembrokeshire; so much has been made of the concentrations of migrants recorded on the islands that the same happenings on the mainland are often overlooked.

We know winter is upon us when the divers appear around the coast. The Red-throated and Black-throated usually do not stay but the Great Northerns are as much a part of the winter as are the Bottle-nosed Dolphins and Herrings. The Herons move down into the estuaries and Kingfishers search rock pools for gobies. The Greenshank, Blackcap, Chiffchaff and Lesser Black-backed Gull regularly stay over, and a Little Egret is no longer quite a rarity. If the birds along the coastal path are more varied and plentiful in winter than in summer, both seasons are exceeded during the migrations of spring and autumn. All through the year the walker along the coastal path will have on his one hand the birds of the sea and on his other the birds of the land. Very few localities in Britain rival the variety, and perhaps only the north coast of Norfolk exceeds it.

St. Bride's church.

Signs of man along the path

All I can do in the space available is to list brief notes
on the types of evidence along the path for man's occupation and use of the coast at different times. No full
account exists of the prehistory or the history of the
county. So the walker who wants to extend these notes
will have to place Pembrokeshire in its regional setting
of Atlantic Britain or even Atlantic Europe. Happily
this would be an exactly relevant study. The concept of
the sea as a way of life unifies the Atlantic promontories
of Europe. Everything came and went by sea; for ten
thousand years the sea was the great provider. The
notion that the sea might be a barrier is brand new in
the west. Until the railways, the sea was the great,
almost the only, means of communication. Now the
railways have almost gone and we depend, foolishly and
in a different way, on the sea again. But political lunacy
could easily cut off the oil supply and, who knows, our
village harbours might be busy once more with something other than the tourist industry.

Mesolithic chipping floors

The earliest signs of man to be seen along the path are
the few sites on which waste material from flint working
accumulated in such quantities that flakes still come to
the surface. These sites date from some ten thousand
years ago, when the post-glacial climate had improved
enough for small groups of Middle Stone Age men to
establish themselves in caves and coastal shelters.
Many of them must have been busy collecting flint from
the beaches where it had been washed ashore by the
waves after falling out of the rotting ice which had
originally collected it up during its advance across
north-east Ireland. This raw material was taken back
by the unskilled searchers to the skilled artists who
made it into scrapers, borers, arrow-heads and spear
20 points. (If anybody doubts that this is an exceedingly

skilful business let him take a flint nodule, any stone hammer or wooden mallet he likes, and try to produce an arrow-head.)

Flint was so scarce that it had to be used sparingly. The tools and weapons were all small: this was a microlithic culture. The waste flakes often contain a face from which four or five other flakes have been struck. Many of these flakes snugly fit between thumb and fingers; only the failure to have a thickness of stone at the back of the working edge prevented the manufacture of another scraper and caused the flake to be added to the pile of waste. Occasionally a slightly towered lump of flint is the remnant core, too small to yield more useful flakes. Anything as finished as an arrow-head is exceedingly rare to find.

Neolithic tombs

Some five thousand years ago a new way of life had permeated up the western coasts of Europe, along which it had been spreading for hundreds of years from its starting point in the eastern Mediterranean. Somewhere in the valley of one of the great rivers man had been improving the greatest discovery he had ever made. The ability to sow in the spring and to reap five- or ten-fold in the autumn released the people from the ever-pressing search and chase after the next meal. These New Stone Age folk were the first farmers. In Pembrokeshire they are remembered almost only by the tombs they built for their dead, several of which occur, if not exactly on the path, then so close that the diversion to see the tomb is simple and rewarding.

Several standing stones, alas, now often more or less collapsed, had across the top a great capstone. The gaps between these stones were filled with dry stone walling, so that a cist was totally enclosed. Over the top was heaped either a long or round mound (barrow) of earth and stones, perhaps to confuse the evil spirits who might have tried to get in. Only rarely are even faint signs of these barrows still visible.

Within the chamber the dead were laid to rest, the knees drawn up to await the new birth. Tools, weapons, food vessels, even parched fragments of corn have come to light, suggesting that the late-lamented were provided with everything necessary for life hereafter.

Burials followed one upon another until the chamber was full. Archaeological evidence suggests that all previous burials were then removed, a bone from each replaced to maintain continuity, and in the space so freed later bodies could be laid. But, even so, burial in these chambers was probably reserved for the higher echelons of society. Ordinary men and women crept away to die among the bushes.

The tombs beside the coastal path are not large. Even so, those who up to now have thought of Stone Age man as no better than a drooling savage might try to work out for themselves how to lift the capstone up on to the standing stones. The Longhouse (Carreg Samson) capstone weighs some twelve tons, others away from the coast much more. The technology of Stone Age man was limited to wooden rollers and levers and perhaps grass ropes. Undeniably they were master craftsmen.

The coastal walker must return to Pembrokeshire to see the marvellous tombs inland. Unfortunately we can show him very little of where these people lived. The site at Clegyr Boia is visible as the path turns its way between St. Non's and St. David's Head.

Bronze Age landing places

Bronze Age man is scarcely seen along the path. In passing West Angle and Whitesand the walker crosses the two places where men sailed for Ireland about 1500 B.C. and continued to do so for some one thousand years, bringing back copper from the Wicklow Hills, to be smelted with Cornish tin to make bronze. Later gold was discovered, for Wicklow to become the El Dorado of the west, and the general journeying doubled and redoubled. The centre of the Bronze power was on what we now call Salisbury Plain, somewhere perhaps in the region of their great cathedral which is now labelled Stonehenge. These were the Beaker Folk. Inland in Pembrokeshire are many more signs of these people, but not along the edge of the coast.

Iron Age forts

On every sheet of the map the path passes through Iron Age forts. Sometimes they are labelled "rath". This is an old Irish word that properly refers only to these embanked fortifications, some built across narrow-necked coastal peninsulas, others inland, on hill-top or steep valley side. Unfortunately, when the surveyors were making the first Ordnance Survey maps they heard the word "rath" but did not distinguish its particular use and applied it generally to any embankments. So that, on present maps, "rath" may be quite misleading: it may refer to some medieval structure or a seventeenth-century civil war fortification.

In the centuries that culminated in Caesar's Gallic Wars, political pressures and a rising population began to force tribes outwards from the centre of Europe. In our case the first wave came up the coast in about 300 B.C. and a later wave some two hundred years later. These people travelled in small tribes or large families; they came by sea, knowing that others were also on the move and that anything they took for themselves they would have to defend.

The first wave built the single straight bank across a narrow coastal neck, with a ditch outside it. The later technique was based on two curved banks and ditches. Anybody trying to rush a gate with a shield on his left arm and a sword in his right hand would hope to make the final attack on a left-hand curve, cutting across the front of his shield. This is the line that is so often denied to the attack by skilful use of ground, perhaps supplemented by subsidiary earthworks, to throw the path at its approach to the gate into a late right-hand curve, so exposing the sword arm side of the attack to the proddings of the defence.

The massive double wooden gates may have been defended from above as well as from the sides. Excavations usually reveal the post holes into which stones have been up-ended to chock tight the posts themselves. A smaller upright stone half-way between the post holes was the doorstop. At some of the entrances the banks are recurved or club-shaped, still further to enhance the defence.

Originally the bank and ditch defence was far more formidable than appears now. Some eight feet or more of material may have slipped from the bank down into the ditch(es). The outer bank was at optimum sling range from the top of the inner. The outer faces would have been as steep as material would stand and in times of trouble a permanent fatigue party must have ensured 23 an absence of toe and finger holds. In fact the whole installation was so strong that almost no evidence exists of any attack. The attackers would have ceased to be a viable social unit after heavy battle casualties. Since any assault would be inevitably a bloody affair the would-be attackers turned aside and found somewhere else to defend for themselves—the first use of the deterrent.

On the defended platform perhaps sixty to eighty people lived in huts—round, dry stone walling faced on the outside with turf to exclude all draught, in the centre a pole to support a roof of thatch, the entrance open downwind towards the north-east, perhaps about ten souls to a hut. Here they lived and farmed out beyond. Among the fields, additional huts would have been occupied except in times of trouble, when all would drive in their cattle and sit out the emergency.

Few of these raths are conveniently close to a stream. Water was stored in clay-lined pits (the principle of a dewpond), supplemented by goatskins (in hot weather, after a fortnight in a goatskin, water must have acquired that certain *je ne sais quoi* to curl the drinker's hair).

Although the path passes through so many Iron Age forts, some of which show individual skill in defensive arrangements of banks and use of changing slopes, only on St. David's Head are the hut circles clearly visible and the original field system still cultivated. This promontory is an Iron Age treasure house, best seen before June, before the bracken submerges so many outlines for another season.

The first Fathers may well have taught the Christian message in these Iron Age positions. How long it was before the raths were finally abandoned is not known. It may be that some were occupied, or re-occupied, as late as Viking times. That would give us the best part of one thousand years of occupation. In any case it is worth pausing to consider that we are today still substantially nearer in time to these Iron Age folk than they were to the people who built the Neolithic burial chambers.

Saints and chapels

Nobody knows when the first Christian message was

carried along the western shores, but the great series of coastal missionary journeys had begun before A.D. 450. Ireland was probably a centre of Christian endeavour before the Word had been widely received in Pembrokeshire. The lines of communication were always and almost only by sea. There was merit in movement in the early Celtic Church; the long missionary journeys were undertaken, not in substantial clinker-built boats of later ages, but in a curragh with a wooden frame covered with skins, a square sail on a mast stepped through the thwart that helped only when the wind was aft of the beam. Otherwise progress was by rowing, using narrow-bladed oars (anyone who has managed a dinghy in a confused sea will know the advantage these narrow blades give).

The same coast, tides and winds and sudden summer squalls that we have to contend with today, lacking our sophisticated aids to navigation, but showing an unshakeable faith in the mercy of God—common prudence prompted those zealous travellers to say their prayers before setting off, and, when/if they arrived, their first thought was a thanksgiving for safe delivery. So from the start, little chapels began to appear along our coasts, dedicated to the saintly leaders.

In the early medieval centuries, the fame of David throughout Christendom brought pilgrims flocking to his shrine. Journeys now started from many more havens and landing places, sailors' chapels doubled and redoubled in number. Saints' names began to multiply along the coasts, eventually to be adopted as place-names, and so on to the maps; as such they persist.

All round Pembrokeshire memories of these journeys survive and of the leaders who inspired them. The very early Celtic Church had within it a strong thread of asceticism, which had come down from the hermits who retired into the desert. Man retreated into the coastal wilderness; there was sanctity in seclusion, not only in single cells but also in small communities. The memory of these retreats is often carried down in the names of saints attached to little islets and isolated rocks. In some cases only the name survives and nothing at all of the man or the activity.

The Age of the Saints (400–800) was in some ways the age of standards and devotion superior to anything

Iron Age fort.

that came afterwards. In the west it was also the age of
continuity.

Lowland Britain had become a Roman province, pro-
tected by the Roman army, with Roman law, clothes,
speech, manners, housing and administration. When
the Romans left in A.D. 410, those living in the lowlands
were quite unable to defend themselves; all that Rome
had stood for, including Christianity, was swept away
by the barbarian invasions from north-west Europe.
The relapse into barbarism, the Dark Ages, lasted until
the revival of learning, led by Charlemagne.

But the Romans never conquered the highland and
Atlantic zones in the same way. Military supervision
was based on a system of roads and forts. No final evidence exists that the Romans ever set foot in Pembrokeshire. Their road turned north from Carmarthen (Mari-
dunum). So when they withdrew they left behind a
people well able to look after themselves. There was no
relapse into barbarism but, in blazing resplendent contrast—the continuity of the life-giving resource of the
Christian way—the great Age of the Saints. The mighty
Celtic Church was only slowly brought to accept the
primacy of Canterbury; eventually in Pembrokeshire

Norman political jobbery masked the true western tradition.

These are the themes that lie behind the many saints' names on the map and the chapels by the path.

The Norsemen and coastal place-names

Evidence for the Norsemen is confined almost solely to the map of the coast. In St. David's, as at Ely, they doubtless prayed, "from the fury of the Norsemen, good Lord deliver us", and little good it did them, for in 987 the cathedral and the foundation at St. Dogmaels were sacked and in 999 the Bishop of St. David's was murdered.

In the eighth, ninth and tenth centuries the Irish Sea was no more than a Norse lake, later dominated from the kingdom established in the Isle of Man. Not until medieval times did the Bishop of Sodor and Man transfer allegiance from the province of Trondheim to York. Many of the bigger places round the Irish Sea have Norse names—Dublin, Waterford, Wexford, Fishguard, Peel—and it is by their place-names that the Norsemen are best remembered in Pembrokeshire. *Holmen* means a small island: Skokholm, Grassholm, Gateholm; the unpronounceable *øy* means a larger island: Ramsey, Caldy, Skalmey (Skomer). *Vik* means a bay with safe anchorage: Goodwick, Musselwick, Gelliswick (not to be confused with *wik*, a cow pasture: Chiswick, Giggleswick). *Skare* means a large rock: Tusker, Greenskar, Gosker. Every sheet of the map of Norway has at least one village called *Dale*. *Angle* means a strait.

Go inland from the path and any trace of the Vikings is much harder to find. We know nothing of where they settled.

The Normans and the great division

Despite the Viking element in their blood, the Normans preferred the short sea crossing to Hastings. The speed with which they spread out is often overlooked. By 1090 they were at Pembroke and by 1110 at Nevern.

The Normans took for themselves the rich agricultural south of Pembrokeshire and defended it with the sweep of castles from Roch to Amroth. While some of the indigenous people went out northwards to maintain their old way of life, they were not evicted. Welsh 27 families continued to own land and grace responsible offices in the south. But the Normans did have to import Irish and Flemish labour to maintain the manorial system, and these newcomers hardened the distinction between the north and south of this county.

The division into the Englishry and the Welshry was so firm when George Owen published his account of Pembrokeshire in 1603 that he could describe a path running through the frontier parishes ("landsker"), as Welsh on one side and English on the other; the girl who married across it was never received back on her own side again.

Nowadays these differences are muted, but anybody taking any part in public debate will soon find they are by no means dead. Along the coast path all one sees are distant views of castles; on the map the language of the place-names changes abruptly at Newgale where the landsker runs out to the sea.

Trade by sea before the Industrial Revolution

All round the coast are ruins, mere rotting remnants, of village quays, piers and warehouses that come to us from roughly the period 1600–1880 (in some cases even as recent as 1914), when every coastal village was engaged in short- and long-distance trade by sea, many of them building their own boats and virtually all of them doing their own maintenance.

The short-haul trades were particularly in coal from Pembrokeshire pits that was distributed round the Irish Sea and Bristol Channel, and in limestone quarried on Caldy, in West Williamston, Lydstep and elsewhere and distributed to the same places. In every sheltered nick in the coast to which there is access for horse and cart stands a limekiln and, near it, the lime-burner's house. Little brigs and schooners came in at the top of the tide, trestle planks allowed the broken stone to be barrowed into the kiln and the burnt lime was shovelled from the shoots below and distributed by cart to neighbouring farms for sweetening the acid soils. In George Owen's day (1600) burning the "kills" was commonplace. The last kiln to burn in Dale was "before the war", but which war is not certain—the

Kaiser's or the Boer!

Some of the ships were literally village shops. On 14 May 1831, a little ship from Bristol tied up at the Parrog at Newport, and, before the locals reached the quay, the crew had displayed for sale hops, prunes, ironmongery, vinegar, grocery, frying pans, soap, candles, chairs, hats, cider, tobacco, brandy, sweets, shot, guns, collars and ties. (The bill of lading has survived.) She would be off before high water to catch the tide down to Cwm-yr-Eglwys, call next day at Lower Fishguard, then perhaps Porthclais, Solva and so work her way back to Bristol for new stocks and the completion of the special commissions the master had promised. In somewhat larger boats other village sailors were engaged in world trade; to Newfoundland for straight building timber, to Morocco for corn, and even round the Horn to the coasts of Chile for phosphates.

In 1848 the *Cradle* advertised passenger berths from Solva to New York: £3 for an adult, 30s for those under fourteen and infants free, for which the ship provided water, fuel and bed places and a warning that the journey might take from seven to seventeen weeks.

From the day the first Neolithic travellers arrived in their curraghs, to the arrival of the railway in the 1850s, all the villages along the coast were in much more direct and constant touch with each other than any of them was with its own hinterland. The railway sounded the death-knell, and the motor lorry, with door-to-door deliveries, killed all this activity stone-dead. But still the walker will see innumerable details from these great days of village seafaring and he may reflect that, where a hundred and fifty years ago a journey round the Horn would pass unremarked in the village pub, there is now scarcely a village boat left that would be seaworthy in winter, and equally few men who could navigate to St. Ives, let alone St. John's.

Milford Haven and the new giants

The oil industry has grown at a speed which passes most men's understanding. Whereas in 1956 only three tankers in the world had a capacity of over 30,000 d.w.t., in 1961–65, 405 others were built and by 1966 half the world's construction was 150,000 d.w.t. or larger.

Fifty feet of water is necessary to float a 100,000-ton ship and this is very rare in the harbours of Britain. The lower reaches of the river Cleddau, drowned by the rise of sea-level as the ice melted, had the advantage of this 50 feet. In 1958, simply because of the underlying geography, the Esso Petroleum Company established the first refinery and B.P. built their ocean terminal from which to pump oil to the refinery at Llandarcy. Since then Texaco, Gulf and Amoco have added their piers and refineries.

Already a 100,000-ton ship is a small one. In 1967 the Harbour Conservancy Board dredged to allow in 190,000-tonners drawing 58 feet and then, in 1968, another £6 million was spent to accommodate 270,000-tonners drawing 64 feet; these vessels are already using the harbour, while 1,000,000-ton tankers are on the drawing board.

The channel is now well into the bed-rock; a further £40 million would blast a channel down to 75 feet.

The economy of size is that in 1972 it cost £2·89 a ton to ship crude oil from the Persian Gulf in a 16,500-tonner, £1·45 in a 70,000-tonner, and £1·10 in a 200,000-tonner. Oil cargoes have risen from 2·8 million tons in 1960 to 17·7 million in 1964, 28·9 million in 1966 and 41·2 million in 1970.

Only about 5 per cent of the refined products leave by road and rail—there is no rail on the south of the harbour—the rest being re-exported in what are light-heartedly called coasting tankers—"little" boats of maybe 30,000 to 50,000 tons. A jointly owned pipeline to the midlands and the Mersey will slice into this part of the harbour's business. Three of the companies pipe fuel to the power station.

When oil is no longer available, for political reasons or because we have used it all up, or if oil is not wanted because a new source of energy has taken over, as may be the case in perhaps thirty and certainly not more than fifty years, only one company will be required by Act of Parliament to clear away its scrap iron. If the precedent of successive governments' attitudes to Ministry of Defence refuse left lying around since 1945 is anything to go by, our grandchildren will curse the day we funked forcing the provision to clean up into the other companies' Acts. But in those days it was not yet respectable to be a conservationist, let alone to look
30 ahead; voices then cried only in the wilderness.

Topographical names in Welsh

The descriptive music of the Welsh topographical place-names along the coast cannot be summarised in a paragraph; much less is there space to translate them all. So much of the romance of their origins, so many winter storms, so many birds and animals and transient incidents in the human comedy and tragedy are now embedded in these words, that a Saxon can only wait patiently for an explanation of the details to come from a Welsh scholar. Who will provide for us the map sheets annotated in this way? Meanwhile I can only quote some of the coastal words, largely drawn from the Ordnance Survey *Place Names of Scotland and Wales*.

aber	mouth of, estuary	carnedd (pl. carneddau or carneddi)	cairn, tumulus
afon	river		
allt	wood, slope	carreg (pl. cerrig)	stone, rock
awel	breeze		
bach	small	castell	castle, stronghold
barcud	kite		
bedd	grave	cefn	ridge
berw	seething water	cei	quay
		cemais	bends in river or coastline
bran	crow		
brenin	king		
bwch	he-goat	ci (pl. cwn)	dog
cadno	fox	cigfran	raven
cae	field	cil (pl. ciliau)	corner, retreat
caer (pl. caerau)	stronghold, fort		
		cnwc	hillock
capel	chapel	coch	red
carn (pl. carnau)	cairn, tumulus	coetan	quoit
		cors	bog

31

craig	rock	maes	open field
(pl. creigiau)		mawr	great, big
crochan	cauldron	melin	mill
croes	cross, cross-roads	melyn	yellow
		moel	bare hill
crug	tump	morfa	salt-marsh
(pl. crugiau)		mynach	monk
cwm	valley	mynydd	mountain
dinas	hill-fortress	nant	brook
du	black	newydd	new
dwr	water	ogof	cave (Ogof Mrs. Morgan: what was she doing there?)
dyffryn	valley		
eglwys	church		
eryr	eagle		
esgob	bishop		
ffos	ditch		
ffynnon	well	pant	hollow, valley
foel	bare hill		
glas	green, blue	parc	field
glyn	deep valley	pen	head, pro-montory, end
godir	steep slope		
gwaelod	bottom		
gwastad	flat, plain	penrhyn	promontory
gwaun	moor, meadow	pont	bridge
		porth	entrance, harbour
gwylfa	look-out point		
		pwll	pool
gwyn	white	rhos	moor, plain
(f. gwen)		rhyd	ford
gwynt	wind	sant, san	saint
gwyrdd	green	traeth	beach
(f. gwerdd)		tref	town, homestead
hafod	summer dwelling		
		trwyn	point, headland
hen	old		
hir	long	twr	tower
isaf	lower	tŷ (pl. tai)	house
llan	enclosure, church	tywyn, towyn	sand-dune
		uchaf	higher
llethr	slope	ynys	island
maen	stone	(pl. ynysoedd)	
(pl. meini)			

Maps reference

		A487(T)
Class 1 Road		
„ 2 „	Fenced B4546	Unfenced
Roads Under Construction		
Other Roads	Good, metalled	Poor, or unmetalled
Footpaths	*FP* Fenced	*FP* Unfenced
Railways, Multiple Track	Station Road over Cutting Tunnel	*FB* (Footbridge)
	Sidings	
„ Single Track	Level Crossing Embankment	
	Viaduct	Road under
„ Narrow Gauge		
Aerial Ropeway	*Aerial Ropeway*	

Boundaries, County or County Borough

„　　　„　„　„　„ with Parish

„　Parish

Pipe Line (Oil, Water)　　　　　　　　　　　　Pipe Line

Electricity Transmission Lines (Pylons shown at bends and spaced conventionally) – ⊗ – – – – – ⊗ –

Post Offices (in Villages & Rural Areas only)　　**P**　　Town Hall　　**TH**　　Public House　　**PH**

Church or Chapel with Tower　**⛪**　Church or Chapel with Spire　**⛪**　Church or Chapel without either　✚

Triangulation Station ＿＿△　　on Church with Tower ＿＿⌂　　without Tower ＿＿⌂

Intersected Point on Chy ＿＿○　on Church with Spire ＿＿⛭　without Spire ＿＿✚　on Building ＿＿▣

Guide Post　*GP.*　Mile Post　*MP.*　Mile Stone　*MS.*　Boundary Stone　*BS* ○　Boundary Post　*BP*○

Youth Hostel ＿＿**Y**　Telephone Call Box (Public) ＿＿**T**　*(AA)* **A**　(RAC) ＿＿**R**　Antiquity (site of)　✚

Public Buildings　　　　　　　　▬▬

Quarry & Gravel Pit

National Trust Area ＿＿＿＿（ Lydstep Point ）
　　　　　　　　　　　　　　NT

Osier Bed

Reeds

Park, Fenced

Wood, Coniferous, Fenced

Wood, Non-Coniferous
　　　Unfenced

Brushwood, Fenced & Unfenced

Glasshouses

Orchard

Furze

Rough Pasture
Heath & Moor

Marsh

Well　　　　　　　　　　　　　W ○

Spring　　　　　　　　　　　Spr ○

Wind Pump　　　　　　　　　*Wd Pp.*

Contours are at 25 feet
vertical interval, shown
broken in built up areas.

Spot Height ＿＿＿＿ *123* ·

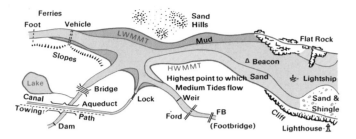

Additional references which appear on the maps in this guide have been drawn
in by the Central Office of Information and the Countryside Commission and
are based on information supplied by the author. These references are:

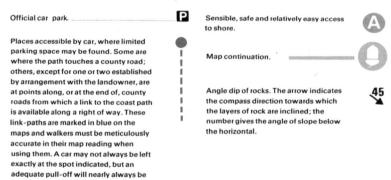

Official car park. .... **P**

Places accessible by car, where limited
parking space may be found. Some are
where the path touches a county road;
others, except for one or two established
by arrangement with the landowner, are
at points along, or at the end of, county
roads from which a link to the coast path
is available along a right of way. These
link-paths are marked in blue on the
maps and walkers must be meticulously
accurate in their map reading when
using them. A car may not always be left
exactly at the spot indicated, but an
adequate pull-off will nearly always be
found within a few hundred yards.

Sensible, safe and relatively easy access
to shore.

Map continuation.

Angle dip of rocks. The arrow indicates
the compass direction towards which
the layers of rock are inclined; the
number gives the angle of slope below
the horizontal.

The line approved by the Secretary of State did not carry the path along the sands between Tenby and
Giltar Point or round Lydstep Head or the Deer Park at the end of the Marloes peninsula. These three lengths
are marked _ _ _ _ _ _ _ _ _ _ _ _ and walkers may use them.

Author's note
The notes which accompany the maps make for easy reference whether a walker is travelling clockwise or
anti-clockwise round the coast. Those who may do only a few miles will, I hope, find the information
equally useful. So many legends refer to the coast, so many figures are shadowy (none more so than the
saints), that my notes are sprinkled with cautionary question marks to warn against jumping to conclusions.

Nothing destroys romance like positive proof; our coast is nothing if not romantic.

1 Coastguard station—disused.

2 The folding that so contorts the dip further south is here
displayed in its entirety.

3 *Dogmael* (Dogfael, Dogwell), fifth–sixth-century Welsh
monk of royal descent. Founded several cells in
Pembrokeshire and Brittany (where he is particularly
invoked for help to children unable to walk) and
Llandogwel, in Anglesey. Original Celtic site chosen by
Norman Robert Martin, Lord of Cemais, in 1113, for a
reformed Benedictine Abbey; two daughter houses, on
Caldy and Pill (Milford Haven).

4 Fulmars.

5 The path by-passes this Iron Age fort.

Pen-yr-Afr.

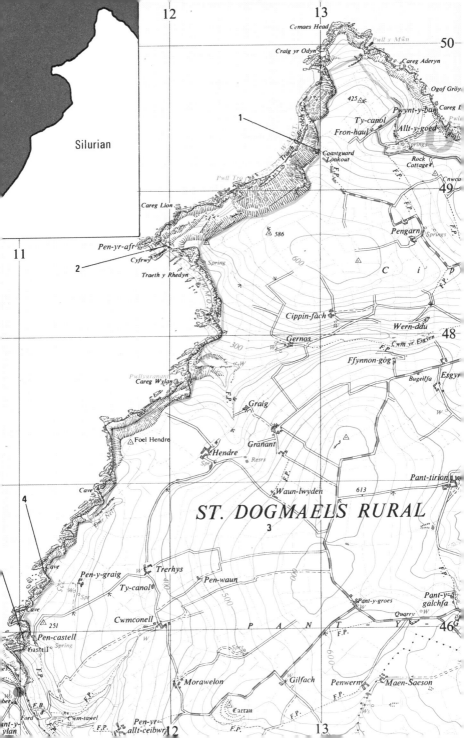

1 *Ceibwr*. Erosion of the bay based on confused and faulted folding, dominated by a sharp anticline. The valley is an overflow channel, massively choked by glacial materials.

2 This flat platform is a raised beach, with rounded beach stones low down in the material at the back of it.

3 Enlarged and collapsed blow-hole; the access arch was the original cave.

4 Iron Age fort with a single curved low bank, with a suggestion of a second bank on the south side: the whole not easily recognised in the confusion of the eroded, slipping cliff and field banks.

5 *Moylgrove*, the Grove of Matilda, 200 acres, part of dowry on her marriage to Robert Martin, first Lord of Cemais.

6 Fulmars.
Pair of Choughs nest hereabouts.

7 Doubt continues about the mass of rock labelled Silurian that comprises the cliffs of Dinas Island and between Newport and Cardigan. The Regional Geology of South Wales says, "the conditions which controlled sedimentation at the close of the Ordovician period continued into early Silurian times without marked change"; but adds a note, "the evidence for the outliers of Silurian rocks west of Cardigan requires investigation". So here is a useful topic for a Ph.D.: Is this coast really Silurian or is it the top of the Ordovician? Fossil, notably graptolite, evidence wanted.

8 Fulmars.

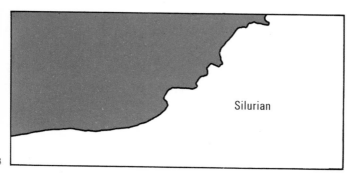

Silurian

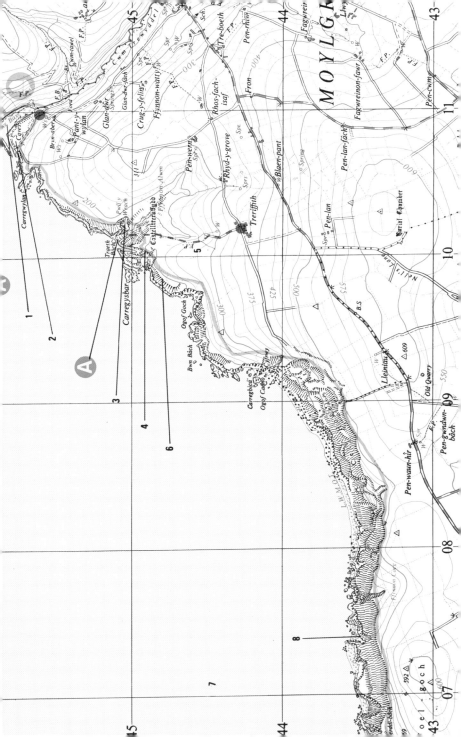

1 Fulmars.

2 The full name of the settlement that preceded Newport
may have been Trefdraeth Edrywy, "the town of Edrywy
beach". This district name may survive here at
Carregedrywy, "the rock of Edrywy".

3 Thirty yards upstream from the road's edge, low in
thick grass, the fragment of medieval masonry is St.
Curig's Well. Site of sixth-century chapel just beyond in
bushes. Newport church originally dedicated to Curig;
the June fair was Curig's Fair. But beware—Curig was a
common name and so it is dangerous to link this site
with Llangurig, etc.

4 Little embankment (maybe Iron Age), ?defended
harbour, ?*c.* 200 B.C.

5 *Newport.* Perhaps the traditional Trefdraeth (the town
on the shore). 1191, Norman William Martin, Lord of
Cemais, driven out of Nevern, established Newport
castle. A charter gave privileges to the burgesses, but
the lordship appointed the mayor and does to this day at
an annual ceremony. Population 1,200; dependent on
tourism.

6 1566, quay at the Parrog was already trading with
Bristol; seventeenth century, woollen exports;
eighteenth century, slates. Coal and limestone imported
and general trading. But always the sandbar was
hazardous.

7 Tree Mallows growing near the café.

8 One-time lifeboat station.

1 At low tide, the best examples of wave-cut platform in
  Pembrokeshire are exposed in these bays.

2 Typical Celtic sailors' chapel smashed by gale in 1859,
  dedicated to St. Brynach, the (?) fifth-century Irishman
  whose work centred on Nevern and whose cult is
  associated with ancient tracks leading to Glamorgan
  and Brecon. He communed with angels on Carn Ingli!

3 Herring Gulls, Razorbills and feral pigeons breed on the
  Needle Rock, and Great Black-backed Gulls on the top.
  On the seaward side a few Guillemots. Fulmars nest on
  the mainland cliff immediately below the path.
  Occasional Shag nest hereabouts.

4 Glacial melt-water channel, the scouring being from
  east to west.

5 I think Castell is a mistake. The apparent embankment
  is geological and not man-made.

6 Glacial overflow channels.

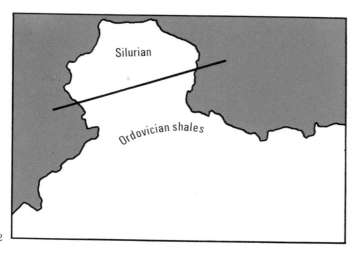

1 Mass of glacial gravels.

2 *Lower Fishguard*, Cwm Abergwaun, was already, in 1566, "a good harbour", trading with Ireland and Chester. In late eighteenth century had some 50 coasting vessels (20–100 tons) in general trade, notably with Bristol. Oats and salted herrings particular exports. Around 1800, small boats built. Spread of railways killed coastal trade.

3 Gwaun valley is exemplar of glacial overflow channels.

4 Monument marking site of French surrender, 24 February 1797, is of Carboniferous Limestone displaying splendid fossils, notably solitary and colonial corals.

5 First lifeboat stationed here in 1822.

6 *Fishguard Harbour*. The 1846 scheme for a harbour and railway was ended by financial trouble and the Irish Famine. Restarted 1899; official opening, 30 August 1906. Steep cliff rising out of 100 feet of water was blasted to provide 800 tons of rock for each footrun of the 2,000-foot north breakwater. Resulting quarry floor becomes platform for harbour and railway installations. 1909–14, Cunard liners called, requiring three to four special trains to a boat; 1908–14 Booth Line and 1910–12 Blue Funnel liners called. Since 1918 only Irish trade, now with Rosslare (54 miles). The Cork trade, which has recently moved to the Swansea drive-on dock, makes Fishguard's future less sure.

7 Visual squalor of suburban fringe starkly contrasts with splendour of uninhabited coast.

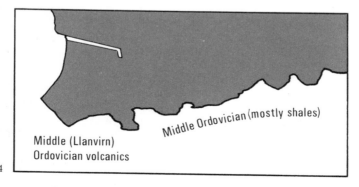

Middle Ordovician (mostly shales)

Middle (Llanvirn)
Ordovician volcanics

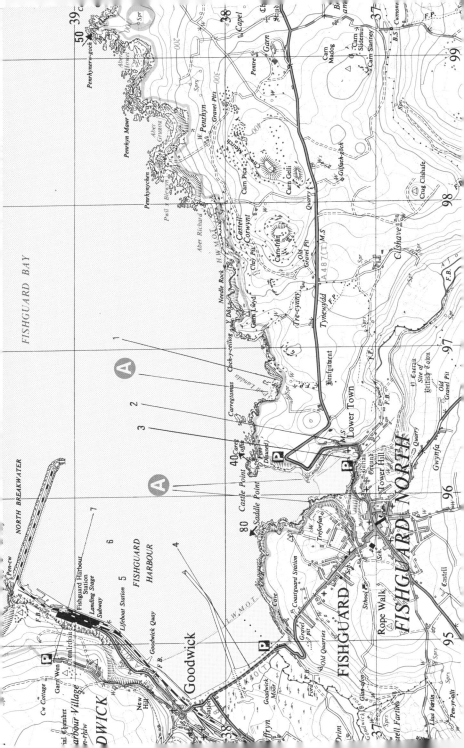

1 Five-sided columnar structure (cf. Giant's Causeway) in cross-section through the dolerite.

2 *Llanwnda* is the church of St. Gwyndaf, who, some say, was the mother of Cybi and maybe sister of Non and so aunt to David; but better authorities say Gwyndaf was a man from Brittany.

3 French diversion, timed with rebellion in Ireland, landed 1,200 criminals and human drift, under an American called Tate, at 5 pm on 22 February 1797, to march to Chester and Liverpool, with 100 rounds of ammunition a man, four days' food and double brandy. The Pembroke Company of Gentlemen and Yeomanry Cavalry, under Lord Cawdor of Stackpole, moved fast. The French drank their brandy and a shipload of wine wrecked a few days before. By 4 pm on 24 February the general surrender was over on Goodwick Sands. Total casualties were eight Frenchmen drowned, twelve killed and one Welsh woman killed in a pub when a pistol was being loaded.

4 A number of small standing stones, each towards the middle of a field, are eighteenth-century rubbing stones for cattle and not antiquities.

5 Typical site of Celtic sailors' chapel on dry ground hard by landing. Around 1750, was partly roofed. St. Degan (Tegfan) (cf. Llandegfan, in Anglesey) has his name here revered in chapel, knoll and well.

6 Large plug of glacial sands and gravel.

7 Pillow lavas low down in cliff section, looking like jumbled heap of rounded bolsters, often in cross-section. These gobbets of lava were extruded through the sea bottom and rolled up by small water movements.

8 Evidence for the coastal movements in the Celtic Church. Cybi was a Cornishman, with two dedications there (Cuby and Tregonny); he journeys north, to Llangibby-on-Usk; to here, Carreg-gibi (Cybi's rock) and then Llangibi, 15 miles up the river Teifi; then Llangybi, near Pwllheli, and Caergybi, the Welsh name for Holyhead.

Middle (Llanvirn) Ordovician volcanics

1 Strumble lighthouse (cost £40,000 in 1908) treated as a rock light by Trinity House. The bridge to the mainland gives keepers the advantages of both rock and shore status. Open to inspection (Tel. St. Nicholas 258).

2 Derelict Ministry of Defence shed would give shelter.

3 Coastguard look-out (Tel. St. Nicholas 613).

4 Derelict Ministry of Defence building would give shelter.

5 *Garn Fawr:* large Iron Age hill-top fort, with multiple defensive walls on east side.

6 By side of farm track, the extreme northern structure, low in bank, is a corbelled cell (alas, with cement added to outside of top). Sometimes labelled "prehistoric pigsty", may be fourth–sixth-century hermit's cell but more likely medieval.

7 Fulmars breed.

8 Choughs breed along this coast.

9 Many Atlantic Seals breed along this coast in September/October.

10 Iron Age fort (?100 B.C.).

11 YHA hostel (Tel. St. Nicholas 233).

12 Memorial stone for Dewi Emrys (1879–1952), whose poem *Pwllderi* is in Pembrokeshire Welsh. The stone for Colonel Madoc, on Langness, Isle of Man, is the only rival I know for simple splendour.

13 Circular, roofless, dry stone wall enclosure; would give some shelter.

14 Headland of the House of the Billygoat.

1 Steep and complete anticlinal fold.

2 Fulmars breed.

3 Long ago, an old man captured a mermaid on Aber-bach and took her to Treseissyllt. She escaped and laid a curse on the house that no child should be born there. One day in 1960 the spell was broken; when the ambulance arrived the happy event had already taken place.

4 Iron Age fort; the inner bank with central entrance; the outer bank has ?eighteenth-century fieldwall built on top of it.

5 Glacial overflow channels.

6 Fulmars.

7 Tree Mallows growing by cottage.

8 Faintly rectangular markings (cf. Gateholm) suggest, not an Iron Age position, still less the resting place of the finger (see 3, p. 52), but more likely early Christian site. Wonderful view of Carreg Samson from the top. Whole stack full of flowers.

9 *Cwm Badau* (Bay of Boats), Abercastle. First mentioned in 1566 as safe harbour. In 1811 sloops based here were trading with Bristol and Liverpool. In 1920s oats were still being exported and coal imported. Two cannon-like bollards survive from those days. The limekiln is in particularly good condition. The "harbour" is a drowned valley.

Neolithic burial chamber.

1 Igneous rocks low down at sea-level have sediments above them folded into an acute syncline which is eroded at its sharpest folding to form text-book little arch.

2 Iron Age fort. Signs of third bank inside outer two. Outer ditch seemingly hewn out of rock, but this may be simply skilled use of geology.

3 Superb New Stone Age burial chamber, *c.* 3000 B.C. The story is that Samson placed the capstone in position using only his little finger which now rests in its grave (8, p. 50). Some believe that the name Samson may be a memory of the spiritual power of St. Samson of Caldy and Dol.

4 Mill-stones still in mill; inspired Archdruid Crwys's *Melin Trefin.*

5 Fulmars nesting.

6 Fulmars nesting.

7 *Porthgain harbour.* Stone was crushed here by 1878. Harbour enlarged and trade vastly increased after 1900 when metalling of roads had become general. In June–August 1909, 101 shipments (13,000 tons) in fleet of six specially built 350-ton coasters. Remnants remain of crushers, binns and shoots. Bricks for their construction baked on site; later exported, notably to Llanelli and "seconds" to Dublin. Thirteen shipments in 1931 were last loads.

8 Navigation marks; this entrance is hard to see from off-shore.

9 Roadmetal quarries in small Ordovician igneous intrusions.

10 Path down to shore is through unusual thickness of glacial deposit.

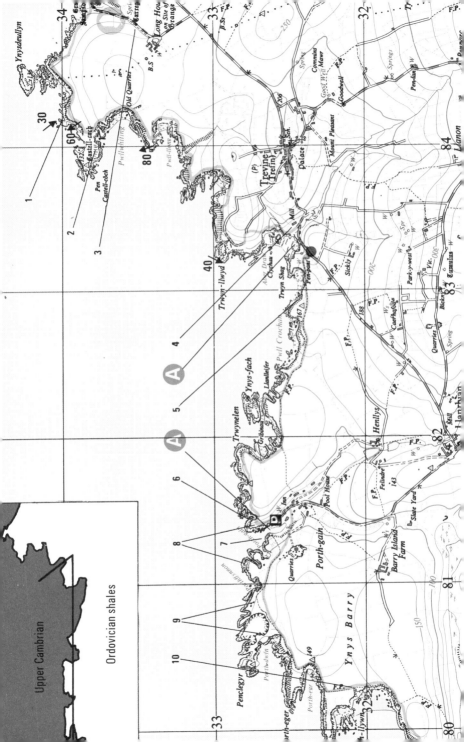

1 St. Barre (Finbar) is said to have sailed from here to
 found Gouganebarra and the city of Cork, from where
 Columba, after a quarrel with Barre, sailed in penitence
 to Iona. Another legend makes Fowey the starting place.

2 1850–1904, the quarry exported slates via a tramway to
 Porthgain, mostly round Bristol Channel and to S.
 England, but railway distribution from N. Wales
 quarries killed this site. Then fishermen formed harbour
 by blasting passage from sea. Now they too have almost
 gone. In north wall of quarry, note near-vertical fault.

3 Maybe a nineteenth-century beacon-navigation mark.

4 Iron Age fort that maybe has complications of defence
 added to an earlier simple embankment in NE sector.

5 Blow-hole.

6 Slate quarry used by nearby farms.

7 Eroded double-banked Iron Age fort.

Fossils in Ordovician Rocks.

Bala Series: 1 *Diplograptus multidens*. 2 *Orthograptus truncatus*.
3 *Dicranograptus brevicaulis*. Arenig Series: 4 *Tetragraptus serra*.
5 *Didymograptus hirundo*. Llanvirn Series: 6 *Didymograptus murchisoni*.
7 *Didymograptus bifidus*. Llandilo Series: 8 *Ogygiocaris augustissima*.

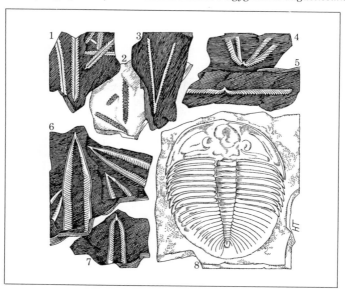

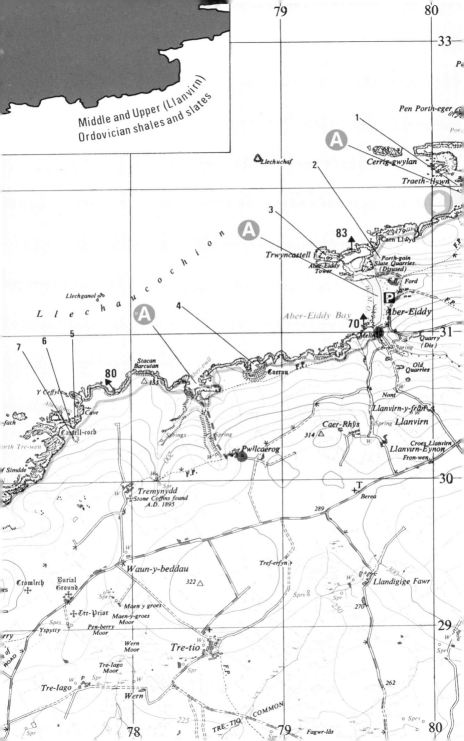

Middle and Upper (Llanvirn)
Ordovician shales and slates

Pen Porth-eger

1

Ⓐ

Cerrig-gwylan

Por...

Traeth-Hywn

△Llechuchaf

2

3

Ⓐ

83 ▲

△179

Carn Llwyd

Trwyncastell

Aber-Eiddy
Tower

Porth-gain
Slate Quarries
(Disused)

B. Ford

P

Aber-Eiddy

Llechganol ⚲

4

Aber-Eiddy Bay

70 ▲

Melin

Spring

Quarry
(Dis)

L l e c h   a u   c o c h i o n

31

Old
Quarries

5

Ⓐ

Nant

Caerau

F.F.

Llanvirn-y-frân

Spring   Llanvirn

7

6

Stacan
Barcutan

Spring

Caer-Rhys

80 ▲

△ 155

314 △

Croes Llanvirn

Y Ceffyl

Llanvirn-Eynon
Fron-wen

Cave

Pwllcaerog

...fach

Castell-coch

-rth Tre-wen

Springs

Spring

W

F.P.

W

30

Spr

T

Tremynydd
Stone Coffins found
A.D. 1895

289

Berea

Tref-erfyn

W

W

Cromlech

Burial
Ground

Waun-y-beddau

322 △

Llandigige Fawr

300

Sprs

270

Tre-Prior

Maen y groes

250

Maen-y-groes
Moor

Pen-berry
Moor

Yspytty

Sprs

29

...rry

Wern
Moor

Tre-tio

ROAD

Tre-Iago
Moor

Tre-Iago

P

Wern

TRE-TIO   COMMON

262

78

225

79

Fagwr-lâs

80

1 Choughs breed along these cliffs.

2 The outer defensive wall of the Iron Age fort, cunningly aligned along an abrupt change of slope.

3 Coastguard on 24-hour watch (Tel. St. David's 210).

4 Neolithic (3000 B.C.) burial chamber.

5 *Clawdd-y-Milwyr* (The Warriors' Dyke); Iron Age fort defended by a wall; courses of dry stone walling visible in entrance and clearly on outer face of north end of wall. Inside are eight circular huts.

6 The virtually inaccessible Cave of Crystal from which fine quartzspar derives.

7 The earliest records refer to "The Promontory of the Eight Perils" which are the off-shore igneous rocks. "The Bishop and his Clerks preach deadly doctrine to their winter audience"—George Owen, 1595. South Bishop light was first lit on 28 June 1838, day of Queen Victoria's coronation. The Crimea transport *Morna* was lost on the North Bishop in 1854, and the Houlder line *Langton Grange*, 12,000 tons, in 1910.

Note

St. David's Head. The Celtic Church was dependent upon the sea for nearly all communication. The only intersection of the great N–S route along the west coast of Europe is here, where the E–W route out of the Bristol Channel and lowland Britain crosses over to the south coast of Ireland. Therefore this peninsula was inevitably a focus of Christian activity in those days (400 onwards). *St. David*, born *c.* 520 by St. Non's chapel; son of Sanctus (Sant), who may have been King of Ceredigion and son of Ceredig ap Cunedda Wledig, a shadowy powerful figure in N. Wales; established strict, almost harshly ascetic community in Glyn Rhosin (Merry Vale); legend of journey to Rome with Padarn and Teilo; 540, made bishop; led puritan revival within Celtic Church; overcame Pelagian heresy at Synod of Brefi (Llandewi Brefi, 3 miles SW of Tregaron)—Pelagius denied the doctrine of original sin; died 1 March 589. Medieval pilgrimage to shrine maintained vigour of seaways until more comfortable alternatives arrived, viz *The Canterbury Tales*.

Ordovician intrusions

Lower (Arenig) Ordovician
shales and slates

1 The Hydrophone Station, 1914–18, housed anti-submarine listening apparatus. Has survived as a holiday house.

2 The irregular field system round Carn Llidi and across the valley is Iron Age in origin and unique in Britain. Here is continuity of 2,000 years of agriculture.

3 This sixth-century sailors' chapel, 13 ft. × 30 ft., for prayers before and after a voyage, is dedicated to Patrick. This is one of several sites along the western coasts from which Patrick is said to have started on his last voyage to Ireland.

4 A Bronze Age (1500 B.C.) track from lowland Britain (Salisbury Plain, Stonehenge), via the Presely Hills, ended at Whitesand, then by boat to the Wicklow Hills for copper and, later, gold.

5 Justinian (Stinan), hermit, born Brittany, reputed friend of David; murdered on Ramsey, walked across Sound with his head in his arms; was buried at site of chapel until his remains were taken into the cathedral. Celtic oratory replaced by present structure by Vaughan, Bishop 1509–22. Bells, stolen by Puritans, were lost in wreck in Sound, now chime only during great gales.

6 Lifeboat house and slip, built 1911–12 for £3,000 (Tel. St. David's 215).

7 Double-banked Iron Age fort.

8 *Ynys Dewi* (David's Island) or Norse Ramsey (some say Island of Garlic, ie Rams-øy; 1548, Turner gave Ramsey as location for ransoms or garlic. Chives still grow on St. David's Head). Legend says 20,000 saints are buried there. Island is now overseen by Royal Society for the Protection of Birds, but colonisation by rats has led to relative scarcity of ground-nesting birds. Seals breed in many caves. Access is from Porthstinan.

9 *Ffynnon Ddewi*—David's Well, where the saint was baptized by Elvis, Bishop of Munster, "who at that instant by divine intervention was landed there from Ireland".

Middle and Lower Cambrian

re-Cambrian intrusive granite

e-Cambrian volcanics (ashes)

Ordovician Basic intrusions

28

74

Carn-hen

Carn-twlc

Carnllidi Bychan

Llaethdy

F.

Sprs

Maen
Sigl

Porth-mawr

73

F.P.

Cave

65

raig y Creigwr

Willioc

Ty-gwyn

St. Patrick's
Chapel

Ffynnon-Fai

Trwynwrddyn

2

1

P MENAPIA
ROMAN STATION

Y

72

PORTH-MAWR

BAY

3

ROMAN ROAD
Supposed Site of

The Burrows
or
Tywyn

A

70

4

Carreg-gafeiliog

A

50 Ogofgolchfa

Carn
Llwyd

Tir-bar

239

Carn
Croeswdig

6

150

26

139

Maen Cam
Ogof Cwm

Cave

Porthselau

139

Croeswdig

Sprs

Springs

55

Point St. John

Penrhyn Dalar

N.T.

Pencarnan

Sprs

100

Treleddyn

Carn Poeth

Treswni Moor

F.P.

Sprs

F.P.

116

F.P.

Waun-
rhossón

a

Porthcau

70

Porthyn Hyfryd

Porth Brasi

St. Justinian's
Chapel
(In Ruins)

P

Ynys Dinas

Rhosson

Rhosson
Farm

N.T.

Carn
Trefeiddan

Trefeiddan

Castell

Clegyr-Boia

25

Bae Ogof Hen

93

Og

5

6

Trefeiddan Moor

F.P.

150

125

136

Ogof Mary

Springs

Castell Heinif

Pen-cnwc

Upper
Treginnis

11

Ford

Rhos-y-cribed

Pen-
Porth-clais

7

Carn
Goch

Carn
Gwil Gelt

Spr

Cave

Rhoduchaf

Ogof Góch

Ogofau Dduon

Carn Fâch

Capel y Pistyll

P

116

Cave

Y Llêch

Rhodisaf

Lower
Treginnis

211

Sar

108

24

Carn-ar-wig

116

Porthllisky

Penmaenmelyn

Melin Treginnis
(Dis.)

Porth-henllys

N.T.

85

Pen Dal-aderyn

163

Porthllysgi Bay

Picrite

9

Shoe Rock

A

Carreg-yr-esgob

72

73

N.T.

74

1 Valley deepened by glacial melt-waters and then drowned by rising sea-level. 1385, cargoes for cathedral; 1566, two 8-ton trading ships owned here; early eighteenth century, breakwater already damaged; around 1910, steam coasters brought coal for gasworks.

2 Non was David's mother and here, legend says, he was born during a great gale. Water in the well soothes almost all troubles. In SW corner of chapel an inscribed cross might date from David's time.

3 Path crosses plum-coloured (jasper) Basal Conglomerate of Cambrian.

4 Arch.

5 Sites from which much of the stone was quarried to build the cathedral.

6 Iron Age fort, unusual in having four banks; entrance on east side.

7 May have been Bwdy = Buite, friend of Teilo; died 521 (cf. Llan-boidy in Carmarthenshire).

8 Massive (?Armorican) fold in the purple Caerfai Sandstone of the Lower Cambrian, faulted against the green-grey sandstones of the Solva Beds (Middle Cambrian).

9 Compact small group of houses: a "clachan", typical of early Atlantic Celtic settlement pattern.

10 South end of the mysterious Monks' Dyke (fosse) that crosses to Penbiri. Could be Iron Age or early medieval.

11 Faulted, folded dark shales of Menevian (Middle Cambrian); abundant trilobites half-way up on east side.

12 Imposing Iron Age fort, much eroded, with interlocking banks forcing approach path into S-turns.

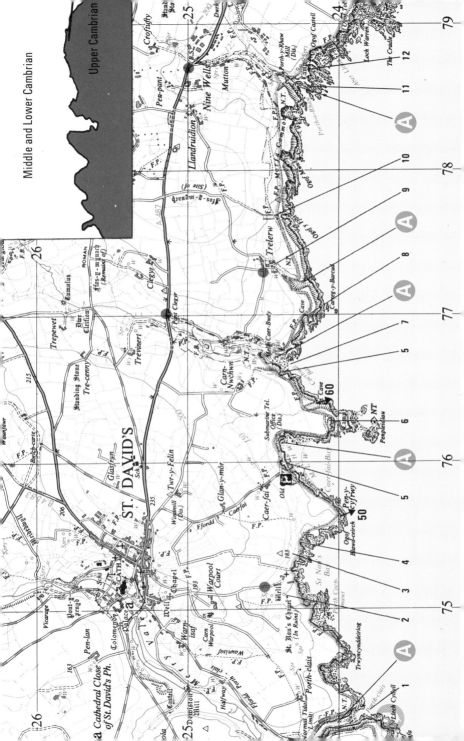

1 How convenient that Tobacco Cave should be just at the end of the track up to the farm!

2 Concentrations of flints (Mesolithic-Bronze) found on surface; the flint derived by ice from NE Ireland.

3 *Solva.* 1536, "creek for ballingers and fishing boats"; 1777, six trading ships; 1820, some 30 trading ships, 20–250 tons; 1851, population 1,252, nine warehouses; 1856, one trading ship; 1901, population 730; 1951, 836.

4 Both valleys are glacial overflow channels, gouged out by melt-water flowing south from rotting ice. As sea-level rose, valley drowned (cf. Milford Haven).

5 Iron Age fort with the original walling visible on north face.

6 Fulmars nesting.

7 St. Elvis was Ailbe, Bishop of Munster, said to have foretold David's fame when the saint was given to him by David's father to be reared by Ailbe for God. Parish population, 1841, 34; 1921, 10; 1951, 3.

8 Fulmars nesting.

9 Many small Mesolithic-Bronze flints found all round this bay.

10 Pointz Castle named from Ponce, an eleventh-century tenant of the Bishop of St. David's.

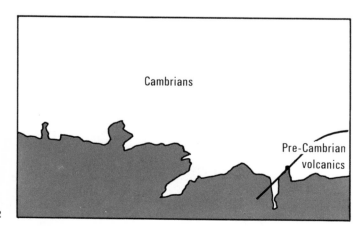

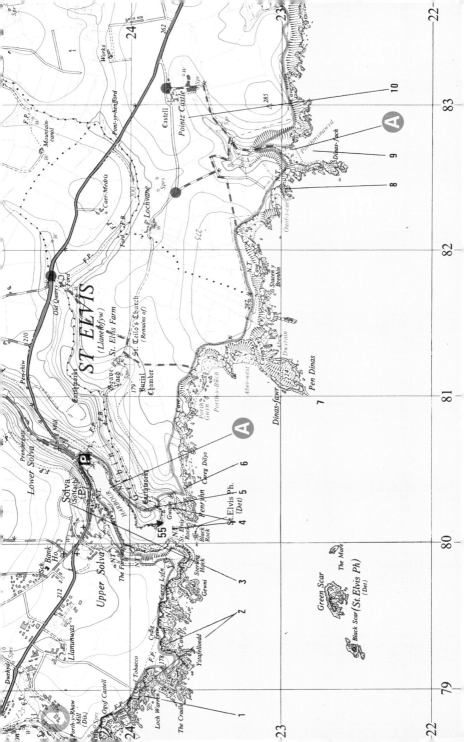

1 This is another area in which the drowned forest has appeared, notably in the winter 1171–72 when "Niwegal Sands laid bare . . . and discovered the trunks of trees standing in the very sea itself".

2 Brandy Brook valley is the west end of the "landsker", the defensive line fortified by Norman castles from Roch, through Haverfordwest, and round to Tenby. This line divides the Anglo-Norman south from the ancient Welsh north (cf. change of language on the maps, notably of coastal features).

3 Pebbles worked by water from St. David's coast are thrown ashore by waves. Top of bank is storm level; successive lines on seaward side mark gradation of high-tide levels.

4 Lifeguard station.

5 In 1124 Caradoc's body, en route for burial in St. David's (north transept), was laid on the ground as the bearers sought shelter from squall. They emerged to find the silk shroud and Caradoc under it quite dry. The chapel marks the site of the miracle. Several years later William attempted to remove a finger as a relic for Malmesbury but "by a species of holy galvanism, the saint suddenly withdrew his hand".

Golden Samphire.   Greater Knapweed.   Viper's Bugloss.

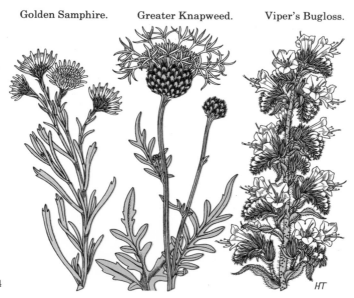

HT

BRAWDY

House

Old Quarry

Troed-y-rhiw

Crûg

Foxen

Parkhole

Bryn-gwyn

Vic.

Leckalee

Rhyd-y-gele

Silver Hill

Tre-newydd

Scarborough

Springs

Brawdy Ho.
Remains of
Manor House

Camp

Crow Cwm

Pen-y-cwm
(P)

Quarry

Cwm Mawr

Llethr
Remains of
Manor House

Blaen-llyn

Old Shaft

wm-bach

Pwll-march

Newgale Farm
On Site of
Manor House

Quarry

Newgale

Brawdy Brook

F.B.

Gouts

Air
Shafts

Pontpren

Old Shafts

Inn

Wood

Wood Farm

Mine
(Disused)

P

West Hill

Southwood
Lodge

Southwood

Longhill

Cambrians

Pinch Hill

The Pinch

Quarry

Midway

Old Shafts

Oxland

Sibbernock
Point

P

Church Hill

Bathesland

Chapel

Druids' Stone

Church

Coal Measures
–shales and
sandstones

Maidenhall
Point

Cave

Bathesland

Old Shafts

Folkeston
Moor

Trefran

Welsh Road

Old
Shafts

Cliff

1 Coal workings hereabouts date back to 1439; Trefrane Cliff colliery was the biggest. Worked from about 1850 to 1905, 300-feet deep and slanted under sea. Coal was first exported from Haverfordwest quay and later in pairs of 8-ton trolleys by traction engine to Nolton Haven and so by sea. At Newgale-Nolton and under sea are some 230 million tons of unworked reserves.

2 Zigzag tracks down to mines.

3 "Old-town." Export of coal by sea was administered from the Counting House.

4 Igneous boulders here are erratics dropped from melting ice. Many more all along this coast.

5 The fault between the Coal Measures and Bala Shales has a throw of 6,300 feet. Line of path down to shore is over masses of glacial "head" in which are marine shells of animals still living in the Arctic.

6 A knight of Henry I (c. 1110) established Drue's ton.

7 *St. Bride.* Tradition of mythical fire-goddess Brig or Brigid was continued in the historical Brigid of Kildare (c. 450–525), a "greater" saint who prepared Ireland's Golden Age; she was the first to become an abbess with authority over a bishop in running jointly a nunnery and a monastery for corporate work and worship. Never left Ireland but her cult was carried to Wales (seventeen dedications), Cornwall and Brittany during Irish movements of fifth and sixth centuries, and so on to Cologne (eleven dedications in that diocese), Italy and Czechoslovakia. Above all she was joyful. Her feast day is 1 February.

8 Line of original Neolithic or Bronze Age track linking landings at Monk Haven (St. Ishmael's) and Whitesand (St. David's). This "Welsh Way" cuts off the dangers of voyaging round the headlands.

9 Natural arch.

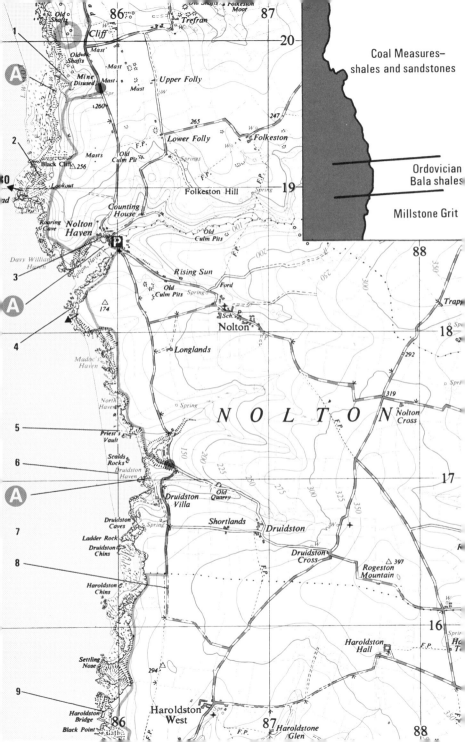

Coal Measures— shales and sandstones

Ordovician Bala shales

Millstone Grit

1

2

3

4

5

6

7

8

9

Ⓐ

Ⓐ

Ⓐ

Ⓐ

86   87   20

88

Trefran

Cliff

Old Shafts

Mast

Old Shafts

Upper Folly

Mast

MINE Disused

Mast

Mast

Spr

260

265

247

Lower Folly

Folkeston

Old Culm Pit

Springs

Wo

Masts

Black Cliff   256

Lookout

F.P.

F.P.

Springs

Folkeston Hill

19

Spring

80

ad

Counting House

Nolton Haven

Roaring Cave

Old Culm Pits

Davy William Haven

Nolton Haven

P

174

Rising Sun

Ford

Old Culm Pits

Spring

Sch.

P

Nolton

88

Trap

18

292

319

Nolton Cross

Longlands

Madoc's Haven

North Haven

N O L T O N

Priest's Vault

Scalds Rocks

Druidston Haven

150

200

225

250

275

300

325

350

17

Druidston Villa

Old Quarry

Shortlands

Druidston

Druidston Caves

Spring

Ladder Rock

Druidston Chins

Druidston Cross

Rogeston Mountain   397

Haroldston Chins

16

Haroldston Hall

Ho T

Settling Nose

294

Haroldston Bridge

Haroldston West

Black Point

86   87   88

Haroldstone Glen

1 Vast landslide in progress. In 1950 one could step across the south end of the crack. The Iron Age fort, according to legend, was the store from which Boia shipped booty and captives to Castell Boia (St. David's).

2 Fulmar colony.

3 These "Harold Stones" mark legendary sites of victories by Harold over the Welsh. More likely Bronze Age.

4 Very tight asymmetrical up-fold (monocline), faulted on its north side.

5 Pembrokeshire Countryside Unit.

6 Inshore lifeboat (Tel. Broad Haven 328).

7 Base of harbour beacon.

8 Coal seams high in cliff face.

9 Iron Age fort.

10 Sixteenth–eighteenth-century mines (collapsed pits).

11 Badger sets.

12 Hazel/oak wood may be one of the very few remaining parts of the original woodlands.

13 Erstwhile lifeboat station; the only shelter in all St. Bride's Bay from all weathers.

14 Lines of ash trees visible in the nineteenth-century plantings; some spindle trees—one of the few Pembrokeshire locations.

15 See how the topography and aspect control vegetation.

1 Iron Age fort; inner bank continues far down slope.

2 Iron Age fort, single bank and central entrance. Immediately under the north end is the junction of the Pre-Cambrian with the Old Red Sandstone; the path changes colour in 200 yards.

3 See how the hard, irregular Pre-Cambrians rise high above the flat-topped Old Red; rocks controlling scenery, as they so often do.

4 Grey blocks lodged in the cliff top derive from melting ice—glacial head.

5 Fine-grained grey near-granite block split in two has been dropped from the ice—an erratic.

6 In cliff section, 10–20 yards north of limekiln, small stone coffins dating from sixth to tenth century appear as erosion proceeds.

7 During nineteenth century, the Edwardes family from Sealyham added the Barony of Kensington to their Irish title (hence Edwardes Sq., Marloes Rd., etc., in London, W.8). This former family seat is now a hospital for old people.

8 The site of a famous Mesolithic chipping floor where, 10,000 years ago, skilled artisans fashioned tools and weapons from flint, worked fragments of which may still be found.

9 A blow-hole. During great winter gales jets of spume burst up from the sea and enlarge the hole.

10 Iron Age fort, unusual in that the single bank is curved. Small stone pits in the living platform could be mistaken for hut sites.

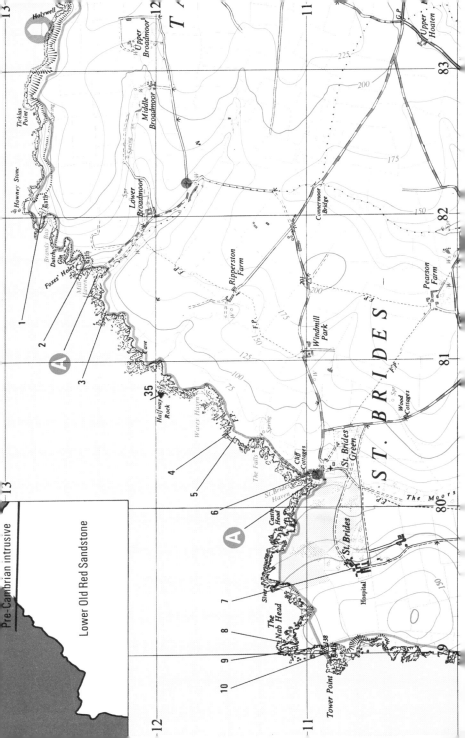

1 Fulmars nest along these cliffs.

2 The Skomer Volcanic Series of the Silurian has within
   it some rocks (Marloesite, Skomerite) found nowhere
   else. Complex faulting includes parallel groups which
   have here produced four rift valleys, separated by horsts
   (square headlands).

3 *Deer Park* was planned as an embellishment of the
   Edwardes estate. No evidence that deer were ever
   introduced, less still that they would have survived.

4 Unusually long early Iron Age fort (*c.* 300 B.C.).

5 One of the few Iron Age forts to have water
   conveniently to hand.

6 *Albion Sands.* The *Albion* was the first paddle-steamer
   to be bought by a Bristol Channel port and was wrecked
   (?1840) here on her delivery trip. Part of her machinery
   projects at low tide.

7 Rectangular huts, largely arranged round three sides of a
   courtyard, may have been Christian monastic settlement
   (*c.* 600).

8 Way up.

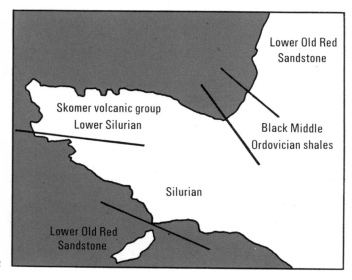

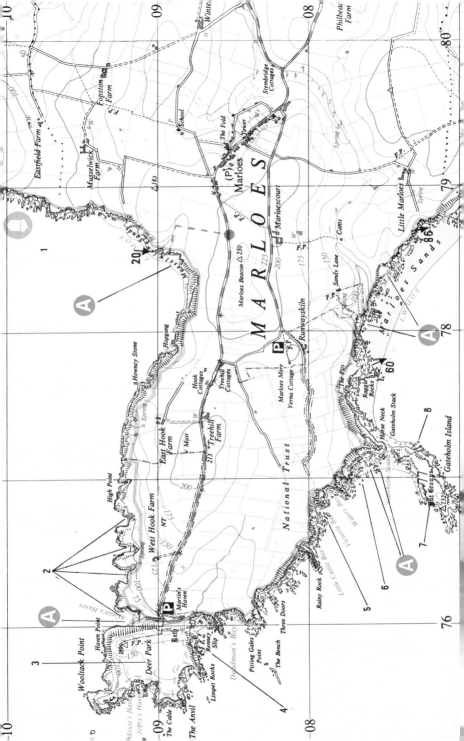

1 The boat for Skomer leaves here daily 10.30 a.m., May–September.

2 Coastguard look-out, rough weather only (Tel. Dale 212).

3 *Skomer* is a National Nature Reserve owned by the Nature Conservancy and leased to the West Wales Naturalists' Trust who raised half the purchase money. The carpets of wild flowers and the colonies of breeding birds (Gulls, Kittiwakes, Fulmars, Puffins, Razorbills, Guillemots, Shearwaters, etc.) compose one of the great sights of British natural history. Day visits from Martin's Haven.

4 Seal pups born here in October.

5 The big spring tides run through the Sounds at six knots, change direction at half-tide and not at full and low water.

6 Choughs nest in this cave.

7 *Skokholm* (see below). The first Bird Observatory in Britain was on Skokholm before the war. Now administered by the West Wales Naturalists' Trust. Visits are limited to those staying at least a week; no day trips are ever accepted. The Edward Grey Institute of Oxford University has a long-standing research programme into the populations of Manx Shearwaters, Storm Petrels and other species of sea-birds.

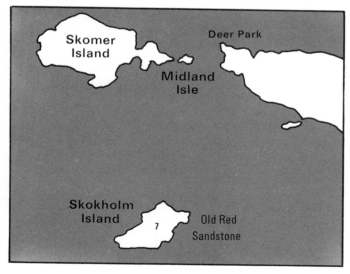

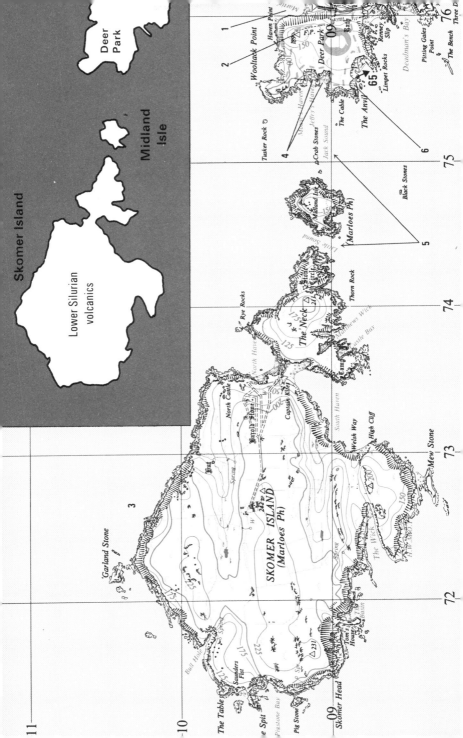

Skomer Island

Lower Silurian volcanics

Deer Park

Midland Isle

1 Before Dale aerodrome submerged the farm these were the buildings of a small holding.

2 The break in the solid rock is due to the Rhaetic fault system which runs from here up the Haven, under Carmarthen Bay and nearly separates the Gower from the mainland of S. Wales. In pre-glacial times the sea ran through the Dale valley and the St. Ann's peninsula was another off-shore island. Then the strait was plugged by material released from the melting ice. This plug is now being eroded again by waves, wind and rain.

3 Later Iron Age fort (100 B.C.). Approach path defensible by clever use of abrupt change of level due to geological faulting.

4 *Dale* is a Norse word, meaning a valley.

5 In 1967 these cliffs were bought by the National Trust with Enterprise Neptune money.

6 Fragments of worked flint occur hereabouts, evidence for the site of a Mesolithic chipping floor 10,000 years ago.

7 Henry Tudor landed here on 7 August 1485, and fifteen days later won at Bosworth.

8 Steps built by Trinity House so that materials for the lighthouse, built 1800, might be landed here.

9 Rock Sea Lavender flowers here.

10 Coastguard station, fully equipped to supervise ships' movements into Milford Haven and to undertake cliff rescue, etc. (Tel. Dale 218).

11 The down- and up-folding, faulted on the landward side, demonstrates in miniature the large-scale folding underlying all the south of the county.

12 Fulmars nest here.

1 Three transit marks help ships to keep in the deep-water channel.

2 Pair of Victorian forts, designed in the days of cannon balls and completed after rifling of barrels and breech loading had already made them obsolete. West Blockhouse, 1857, seven guns "en barbette", two-storied barracks; *c.* 1900 an open battery was built on higher ground and manned until 1950.

3 A great down-fold passes through Watwick, under the Haven and through West Angle; the sides of the bays slope (dip) towards the middle.

4 Transit mark to keep ships in the deep water.

5 Irrigation pond.

6 Early Iron Age fort (?300 B.C.).

7 1856 fort, paired with Thorn Island. 7–10 guns "en barbette"; landward defensive ditch flanked by a caponiere. (The last generation of such forts.) Two-storied barracks; a Field Centre since 1947.

8 The contractors left too narrow a baulk on the seaward side when gravel was dug in 1941/2 to make Dale aerodrome; the sea broke through and flooded the pits. Now the whole shore line is moving inland; already since 1947 two lagoons have been filled up with stones pushed in by the tide.

9 Badger set.

10 The road from Monk Haven to St. David's removes the dangers of sailing round the coast of Pembrokeshire and may have been used in Neolithic times. In the days of the saints and even more during the medieval pilgrimages, this was a busy landing. Vestiges of religious buildings remain. The wall across the shore is eighteenth century and the little tower a folly.

11 Coastal artillery positions from 1914.

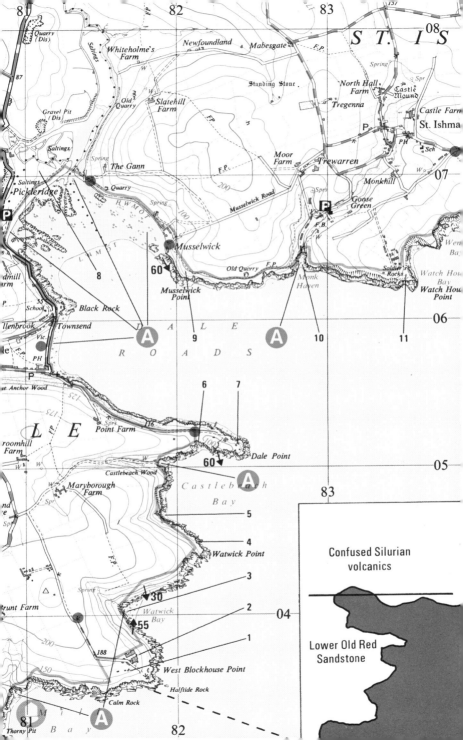

1 Iron Age fort.

2 Transit towers to control entrance to Haven.

3 Dryshod crossing for only three hours either side of low water.

4 Iron Age fort; the outer of the two banks is very small.

5 South Hook fort, 1863. Two open batteries: fifteen guns in westerly and five in easterly. Substantially altered 1900. Defensible barracks capable of mounting guns on roof. Arcs of fire interlocked with Stack.

6 Esso refinery opened in 1960. Present capacity is fifteen million tons, much of which now goes out by pipeline.

1 Ringed Plover. 2 Common Sandpiper. 3 Turnstone.

HT

1 1863 fort. Casemates for eleven guns, plus eight in open
   battery and nine in battery to eastward. Altered 1900.
   Cartridge magazine below casemates; powder magazine
   cut into rock behind. Two-storied bomb-proof barracks.

2 Offices and pier of Milford Haven Conservancy Board
   (harbour master, pilots, shipping control, etc.).

3 *Milford Haven*, started 1810 by Quaker Nantucket
   whalers. 1863, railway came; 1888, dock; trawling
   becomes almost sole support of town. 1950, population
   12,700; fishery collapses; economy only somewhat
   diversified and is too dependent on chance construction
   work for future prosperity to be anything but unsure.

4 Thos. Ward's ship-breaking yard established 1934,
   closed 1956.

1 Large Skipper. 2 Small Heath. 3 Dark Green Fritillary. 4 Small
Copper. 5. Common Blue. 6 Pearl-bordered Fritillary.

1 Gulf opened refinery in 1968; current capacity is five
  million tons of crude oil annually, mainly from Middle
  East sources, brought in 100,000-tonners from ocean
  terminal in Bantry Bay; 60 per cent of products are
  shipped by sea, the rest by road, rail and pipeline.

2 Not Martello (i.e. anti-Napoleon) towers, but completed,
  1857, as inner defence of dockyard, with Pater Battery of
  23 guns.

3 Church dedicated to St. Tudwal, a Welsh monk revered
  also in Brittany, where he died 564.

4 *Neyland*, built 1856 as terminus of Atlantic–Manchester
  railway; but Crosby Sands could be charted after all and
  Liverpool grew. Royal Navy at Pembroke Dock
  obstructed development of Irish trade which went to
  Fishguard in 1906 and fishing fleet to Milford. Neyland
  was born to disappointment; has always had to depend
  upon others to provide it with a living.

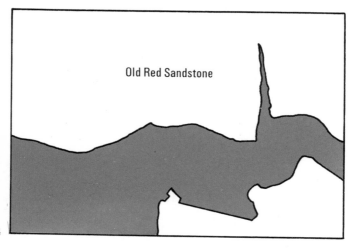

Old Red Sandstone

1 *Pembroke Dock.* 1814, naval dockyard established. Steady progress to 1918. In 1926 dockyard turned over to care and maintenance; about 75 per cent of town unemployed. 1936, dockyard revival; flying boats arrive; Battle of Atlantic. 1950–70, town too dependent on chance construction work for future to be assured.

2 *Pembroke* (Pen bro(g), Head of the Land, i.e. Landsend); castle started in 1090 by Arnulph of Montgomery. Curtain walls and entrance gate include every form of enfilade and obstacle. The inner ward dominated by circular donjon (keep) which was a last resort of defence and proved such a trap that it was abandoned around 1200 (see Manorbier, 1, p. 106). Henry Tudor born here 1457. Cromwell knocked it about a bit, after which the castle walls and town walls were dismantled.

3 *Monkton.* Benedictine priory, dedicated to St. Martin (?of Tours); established 1098 on land given by Arnulph of Montgomery and his successor William Marshall; daughter cell of Sayes, in Normandy, until it passed to St. Albans in reign of Henry VI. Post-reformation decay ended by restoration and *art nouveau* decoration of choir and sanctuary. Visited by Edward VII. Fifteenth-century Old Hall was prior's house.

Pembroke, seventeenth century (from "Wales in Maps" by Margaret Davies, University of Wales Press).

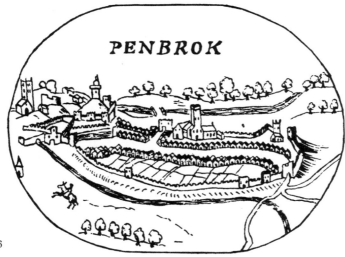

1 CEGB 2,000 MW oil-fired power station.

2 Mussels and other shells by the side of the path have been carried up by crows from the flats below.

3 Texaco oil refinery started up in 1964; some eight and a half million tons of petroleum products are produced annually.

4 Eastern end of Iron Age banks badly damaged by cutting for oil pipes.

5 B.P. terminal opened 1961. Up to eight million tons of oil pumped annually for refining at Llandarcy.

6 1863 fort. Casemates with iron shields for eleven guns and higher open battery for twenty. Remodelled 1900s. Defensible barracks in irregular hexagon. The whole building now houses B.P.

7 Cockles.

B.P. installations, Angle Bay.

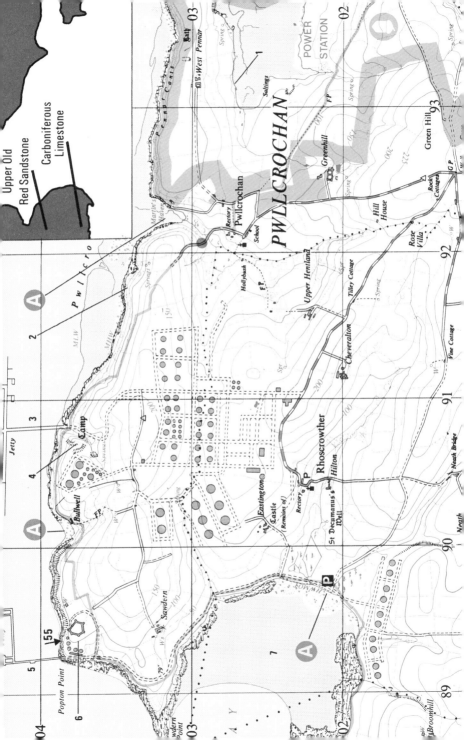

1 An echo of pre-railway Pembrokeshire coast, characterised by rotting timbers of three ships, ruined quay and harbour walls.

2 Lifeboat station (Tel. Angle 204/263).

3 Medieval strip fields survive in present pattern.

4 The Mark 1 open battery was spread along cliffs further east. Fort completed 1870s; notable scale of revetted ditch, flanked by polygonal caponieres, looped for musketry. Open battery remodelled 1900s for heavy guns, with magazines below.

5 Outcrop of coarse Ridgeway Conglomerate.

6 1854 fort; casemated battery of nine guns, improved 1860 to give fire all round. Now a hotel.

7 East Blockhouse, only surviving remnant of post-Armada defences. Nineteenth-century fort was demolished, only battery, dating from 1900, remains.

8 Single-banked Iron Age fort (?300 B.C.), into which in 1914 (or thereabouts) look-out was built.

9 *Angle*, Norse word meaning a corner or turning (i.e. into the Haven from open sea).

10 Single-banked Iron Age fort (?300 B.C.), with causeway entrance on east side; original stone walling still visible.

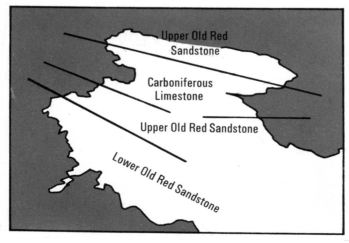

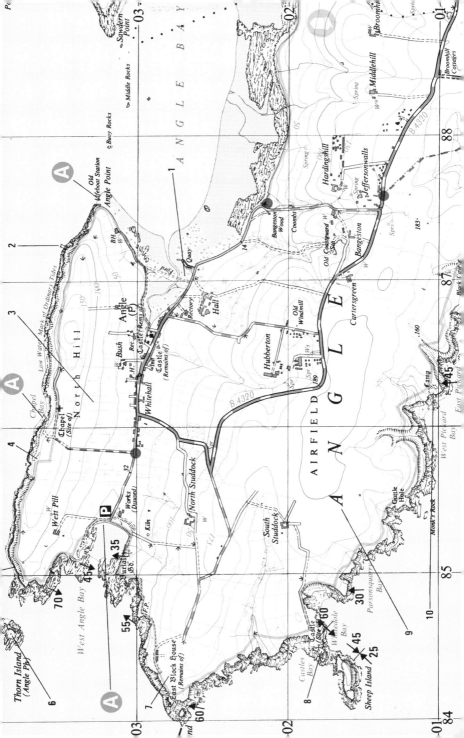

1 Single small stack of very coarse conglomerate which is
the basal conglomerate of the Old Red Sandstone.

Note

At the present time the Army tank range denies access to
the coast from Gupton Burrows to Flimston Down. On
firing days this prohibition extends as far as a gate above
Broad Haven (see 3, p. 100). The walker then has to use
the road all the way between Bosherston and Gupton.
The firing programme is posted at least ten days in advance
in Bosherston post office (Tel. Castlemartin 286) and in the
local papers. On days when firing does not take place, the
splendours between Broad Haven and Flimston are
available to walkers.
I have annotated the entire coastline of the range in
preparation for the day when the Army disappears and we
can walk round Linney Head once more. (See map on
page 95.)

1 Oarweed.   2 Saw Wrack.   3 Bladder Wrack.

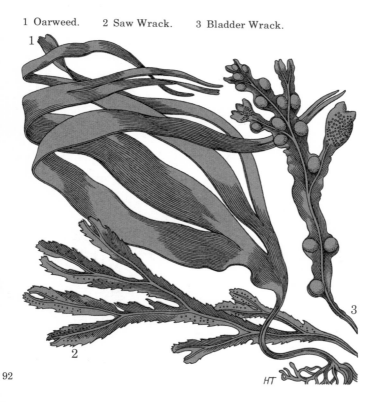

HT

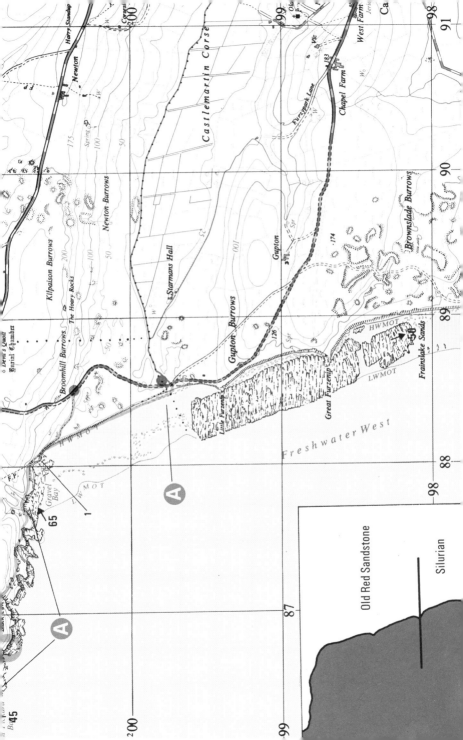

1 Site of forest drowned some 5,000 years ago.

2 View from Linney Head (see inset opposite page).

3 Blow-hole 50 yards back from cliff edge, based on faults along which a deep gut has been eroded.

4 Iron Age fort; central entrance with three banks to west of it and only one to the east.

5 Trinity House maintains the beacon on this dangerous rock.

6 Linney Head to Mount Sion is a length of particularly clear Armorican folding, epitomized in Pen-y-holt Bay, which is best seen from the west side. The sequence from seaward is (i) arch through steep anticline in Cabin Door; (ii) syncline through beach and up to cliff top; (iii) curls over into an anticline which leads down northward into yet another complete syncline. Fossils are common in many places—solitary and colonial corals, brachiopods, sea-lilies, etc.

7 Tree Mallows grow on top of stack; Guillemots nest on its ledges.

8 Wind/salt-eroded cliff top covered by thin layer of rounded glacial pebbles among which Old Red Sandstone (?from Angle) are conspicuous.

See Note on page 92.

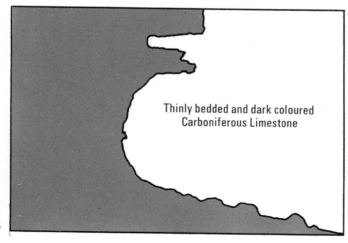

Thinly bedded and dark coloured
Carboniferous Limestone

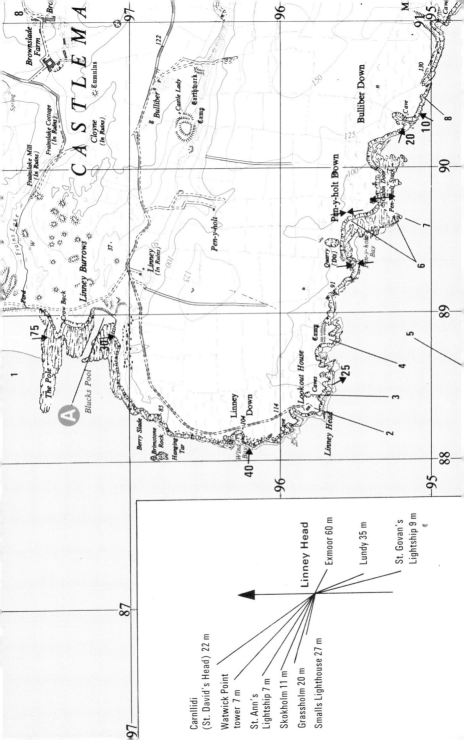

1 *Castlemartin.* Inside the church is a pillar-stone
(?seventh–ninth century) on which a crude cross is
incised; also an organ said to have been made for
Mendelssohn. The "castle" is a Norman motte and bailey.
In 1602, the whole parish was "inhabited by the Irishe,
haveinge not one Englishe or Welsh but the parson". In
1806, Sir John Owen of Orielton won the gold medal of
the Royal Society of Arts for draining marshland. In
1811, Fenton says, "a place worthy the attention of
every traveller, as a specimen of farming brought to a
degree of perfection unexampled in this country".

2 Blow-hole.

3 *The Green Bridge to Mewsford Point.* Where rock falls
are recent and in fissures running deep down from the
cliff top, brown-brick-red staining of the grey limestone
derives from the Triassic marls which have long since
been removed by erosion, particularly by wave-action
when the sea-level was up on the 200-foot platform,
which is so clearly displayed here in the view inland
along the cliff edge.
Contemporary marine erosion is producing caves, blow-
holes, arches and stacks which make Flimston a name
famous among geographers. The underlying weaknesses,
based upon faults and folding, are often quite obvious.
The sea-bird colonies are by far the largest to be seen
from the path. Guillemots occupy ledges and tops of the
stacks, among the Tree Mallows and Sea-beet;
Kittiwakes nest in colonies on steep cliffs, while
Razorbills are scattered under overhangs and in cracks.
Fulmar Petrels on wider ledges are sometimes in full
view. A few Shags nest in larger holes in the cliff face,
which is hereabouts so well coloured by the glowing
orange lichen *Xanthoria*.

4 Iron Age fort with two banks.

5 Gash-breccia (see 6, p. 100).

6 Single-bank Iron Age fort, best seen from the top of the
outcrop inside the fort.

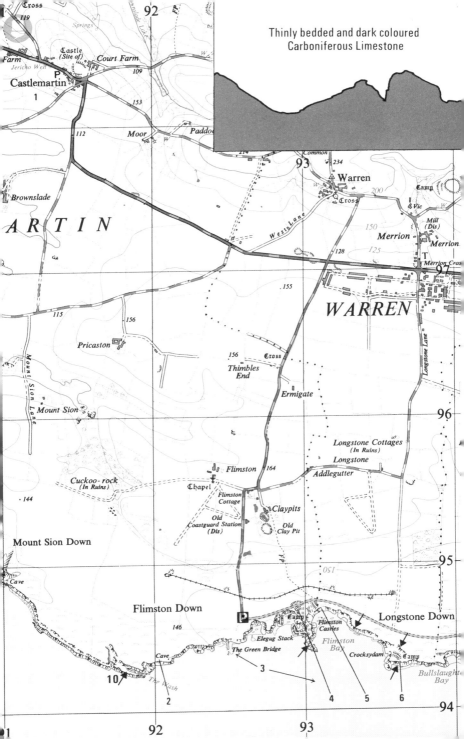

1 Incipient blow-hole within which Ash and Blackthorn flourish, sheltered from the wind and salt. They may constitute the climax vegetation.

2 Iron Age fort, with an outer bank and (more doubtful) inner wall; beautiful military use of the blow-hole.

3 Erosion along a relatively small fault. Used to be called both Penny's and Adam's Leap.

4 Fifth-century hermit's cell; occupancy variously ascribed to: (a) ?Cofen who may have been the wife of a king of Glamorgan; (b) St. Gobhan, contemporary of David; (c) person or persons unknown. Chapel is thirteenth century. Red mud from the Holy Well cured eye troubles; ran dry this century.

Green Bridge.

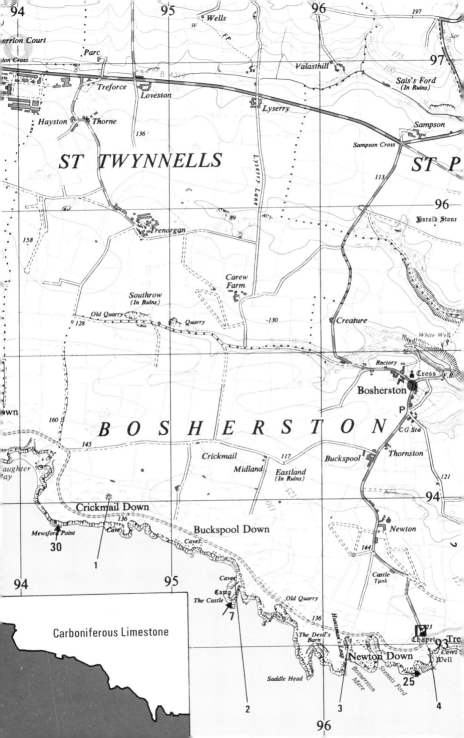

94 **95** **96** **97**

Wells

W   FP

Perrion Court

ton Cross

Parc

B 4319

Treforce

Loveston

Valasthill

Sais's Ford
(In Ruins)

Hayston   Thorne

Loveston

Lyserry

Sampson

136

Sampson Cross

ST TWYNNELLS

ST P

158

Trenorgan

89

113

96

Harold Stone

Carew
Farm

Southrow
(In Ruins)

Old Quarry

128   Quarry

-130

Creature

White Well

Rectory

Cross   F.B.

Bosherston

P

C G Sta

160

B O S H E R S T O N

145

Crickmail

Midland

117

Eastland
(In Ruins)

Buckspool

Thornston

121

aughter
ay

94

Crickmail Down

136

Cave

Buckspool Down

Newton

Mewsford Point

Caves

144

30

Castle
Tank

1

Caves

Camp

The Castle

Old Quarry

7

136

The Devil's
Barn

Chapel   **93** Tre

94   **95**

Caves
Well

Newton Down

25

Saddle Head

Bosverston
Mere

Stennis Ford

4

2   **3**

96

Carboniferous Limestone

1 Coastguard station; rough weather watch only (Tel. Castlemartin 235).

2 House-martins, Fulmars, Shags and Razorbills all breed on these cliffs and stacks.

3 Gate onto tank range.

4 Ash trees flourish in the shelter of this collapsing blow-hole.

5 *Stackpole.* From Norse *stac*, an isolated rock, and *pollr*, a small inlet. Accumulating sand impeded drainage. In eighteenth century, when Earl of Cawdor married Miss Lort, heiress to the 15,000-acre estate, a new mansion was built on the Norman site and the valley was dammed to provide lakes. House was demolished in 1967; the estate continues under Lord Cawdor.

6 Rain and streams percolating through limestone dissolve out caverns, the sides and roof may later collapse, and angular masses are washed in from above to fill up the cavern with "gash-breccia"—unsorted, unlayered and often stained reddish. These filled-up caverns are exposed in the cliff section by present marine erosion.

7 Fulmars breeding.

8 Blow-holes in various stages of development. Air, water, and even stones may burst up during gales through these collapsed roofs of sea-caves.

9 In 1798, Lord Cawdor and his family used to keep their yacht *Speedwich* in this harbour.

10 Elidor—Teilo, alias Eliud, to whom the church is dedicated.

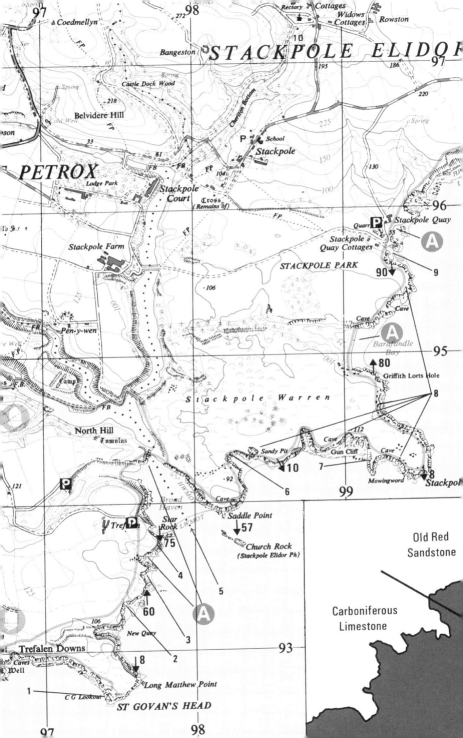

97

a Coedmellyn

272 **98**

Rectory Cottages
Widows Cottages
Rowston

10

Bangeston

STACKPOLE ELIDOR

97

Castle Dock Wood

195   186

Spring

Belvidere Hill
218   Cheriton Bottom   225   220

Spring

Old Well

33   P School   150

81   Stackpole   130

PETROX   104   100

Lodge Park   FB   FB   FP

Stackpole
Court   96

Cross
(Remains of)   FP

Quarr   P Stackpole Quay   Ⓐ

Stackpole
Quay Cottages   9

Stackpole Farm   STACKPOLE PARK   90

106

Pen-y-wen   FB   Cave   Cave

Barafundle Bay   95

Camp   FB   80
Griffith Lorts Hole   8

Stackpole Warren

North Hill   112   Cave
Tumulus   Sandy Pit   Cave   Gun Cliff   Cave

P   10   7   Mowingword   Stackpol

92   99   8

121

Broad
Haven   Cave   6

Ψ Trefn P   Star
Rock   Saddle Point   57

75   Church Rock
(Stackpole Elidor Ph)   Old Red
Sandstone

4

5

60   Ⓐ

3   Carboniferous
Limestone

2

Trefalen Downs   93

8

Caves
Well   Long Matthew Point

1   C G Lookout

ST GOVAN'S HEAD

97   **98**

1 Fulmars breeding.

2 Iron Age fort with multiple defences that may include the enlargement of the original position.

3 The visual squalor produced by shack development before the designation of the national park was one reason that determined plans for a small resort here. The cumbersome planning machine has lurched this way and that for ten years without producing a decision. Meanwhile the environment is despoiled and the sand-dune habitat destroyed.

1 Spring Squill. 2 Sea Campion. 3 Sea Pink. 4 Cross-leaved Bell Heather. 5 Bell Heather. 6 Ling (Heather).

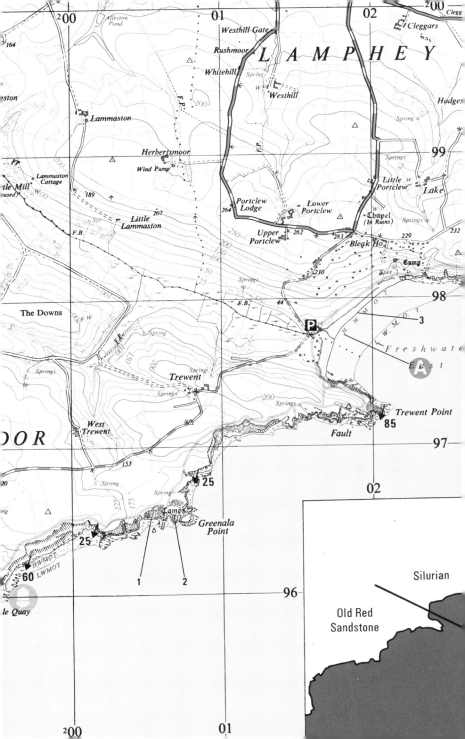

1 The skill in siting this little Iron Age fort is apparent
only when standing on the top of the inner bank. The
slopes are surprising. The fort is being rapidly destroyed
by erosion, from human feet mainly.

2 Geological irregularities give an impression of
embanked defences.

Large waders: 1 Bar-tailed Godwit (autumn-winter dress). 2 Oyster-
catcher. 3 Curlew. 4 Whimbrel. 5 Redshank.

HT

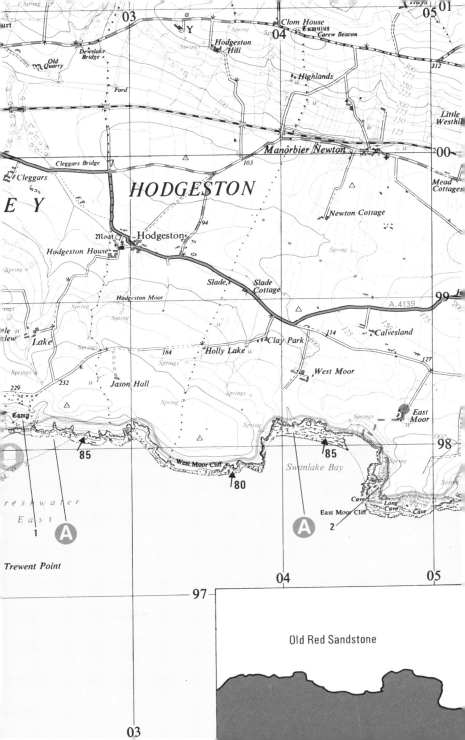

1 *Manorbier, c.* 1188, known as Maenor Pyr—the manor
of a man called Pyr (see Caldy, 12, p. 108). In fourteenth
century simply Beere.
Manorbier Castle. At the end of twelfth century
improved techniques of fortification led to simplification
of the defence, with a reliance upon a single wall of
enceinte and round flanking towers. The large courtyard
made possible the lord's luxurious domestic
accommodation.
Giraldus Cambrensis born here 1146(7), son of Norman
noble and Welsh princess. Despite fiercely military
family, entered church; became archdeacon of Brecon.
King John repeatedly refused him bishopric of St.
David's. So Giraldus wrote a series of topographical
books, including *The Itinerary through Wales.* Prompted
Innocent III to canonise Caradoc (see 5, p. 64). Died
c. 1223—reputedly buried at St. David's.

2 Neolithic burial chamber (*c.* 3000 B.C.).

3 Iron Age fort that skilfully includes abrupt geological
changes of level to deepen the defensive height. Inside
are hints of hut circles (*c.* 300 B.C.).

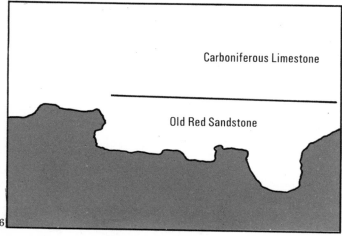

Carboniferous Limestone

Old Red Sandstone

1 Gash-breccia (see Stackpole, 6, p. 100).

2 This flat-based "bay" into the cliffs is one of the raised beaches cut when sea-level was about 20 feet higher than now.

3 Sloops lay in here loading limestone for Bideford, Cardigan, etc.

4 In SE corner of the quarry is a vertical brown stain which probably derived from New Red Sandstone of the Triassic, before that Sandstone was planed off by the sea.

5 "Sweet little cove of Lidstep", Gosse (1886). Would he say that now?
A large down-fold (the Pembroke syncline) here runs out to sea and is eroded to produce Caldy Sound. Note the angles of dip.

6 Blow-hole.

7 Blow-holes, connected to large and deep caves.

8 Incipient blow-hole, exactly as described at the beginning of this century.

9 Dewberry (*Rubus caesius*) common hereabouts.

10 The Round-mouthed Snail (*Pomatia clegans*), common. Not far removed from a winkle, it is at a more advanced stage in the migration up from the sea.

11 Nobody knows the origin of these ruined structures.

12 Caldy (see inset)—In Norse, cold island—Welsh, Ynys Pyr, the island of Pyr (cf. Manorbier). In sixth–eighth century occupied by the saints. Samson, friend of Teilo and David, was Abbot before his missionary journeys which ended at Dol (Brittany); died *c.* 565. From 1113 to 1534 Benedictine monastery; 1906, Benedictines return, but, 1928, go on to Prinknash. Trappist Cistercians arrive from Belgium, 1929.

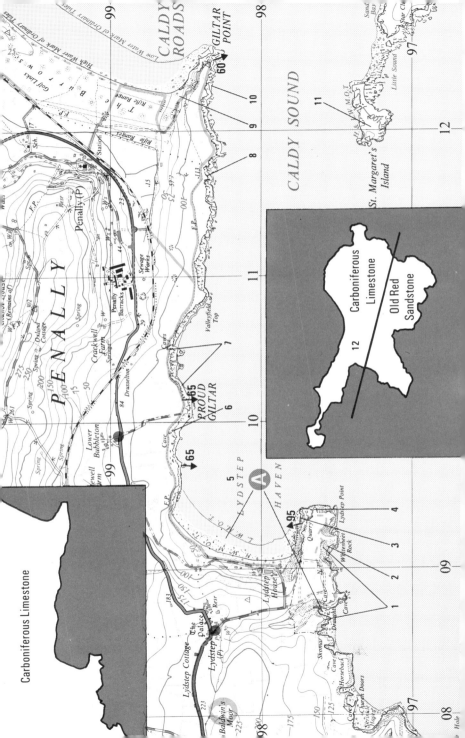

1 *Pen,* a headland. Pre-sand-dune cliffline clear on map and in landscape. Teilo, born Gumfreston, lived as boy in Penally. Friend of David and Samson. Life's work based on Llan-deilo (Carms.). Buried (?) Penally c. 580.

2 Many kinds of shell come on to this beach.

3 Post-glacial bay-bar from Giltar to Tenby is the nucleus of present dunes and led to silting of Ritec valley which in eleventh century was open as far as St. Florence and in 1643 obstructed the Parliament forces. Land reclamation, notably the 1811 embankment on which the railway (1865) ran, and culverting of Ritec, accelerated accumulation of sand which is carried towards Tenby on SW wind.

4 Dunes dominated by Sea Buckthorn.

5 The brutal coarseness of this tall, grey building and its label "Fun Drome" aptly suggest the tone of the tourist development that would overwhelm this coast, if it were not for national park planning.

6 Attractive museum.

7 1868 Victorian fort, contemporary with Haven forts, six guns in casemates; on site of chapel dedicated to Catherine, patron of spinners, a trade in Tenby until sixteenth century.

8 Norse *skare*, a rock; many examples.

9 Tenby?, Dinbych-y-pysgod (the little fort of the fishes). ?Eighth-century Norse settlement; ninth-century Welsh stronghold; twelfth-century Norman castle; thirteenth-century town walls. 1328, breakwater built (the first in Wales); 1566, 200 households (except Haverfordwest, largest town in Pembrokeshire); 1841, 2,912 inhabitants; Georgian/Victorian watering place "of refined excellence"; 1921, 4,830 inhabitants; 1971, 4,750 inhabitants, almost totally dependent on tourism.

10 St. Julian's chapel, built 1878, near what may be a sixth-century or medieval site, dedicated to Julian the Hospitaller, patron of boatmen, also named "the Poor".

11 Coastguard (Tel. Tenby 2031); Lifeboat (Tenby 2597, night 2566).

Continued on page 112

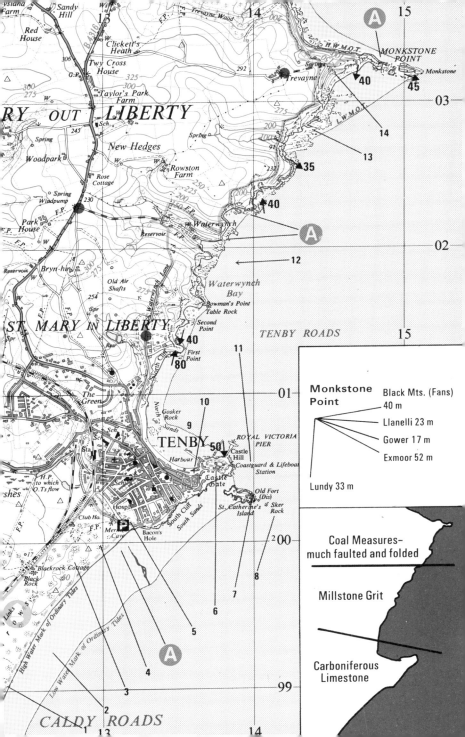

Continued from page 110

12 The most sheltered shores in Pembrokeshire, dominated by woods; scrub oak along the fringe, with some Sycamore. Plantations of blue Sitka Spruce, the dark green pines with clumps of heavy needles, and some Larches, emerald green in summer and soft misty ginger in winter.

13 Expanse of wave-cut platform beneath black shales and ginger sandstones.

14 Coastguard; day watch only (Tel. Saundersfoot 2722).

---

1 Common Polypody fern abundant, with mosses, on older oaks.

2 Strange clumps of *Cotoneaster simonsii* which must have started from berries picked by birds from gardens and dropped.

3 Hairy Woodrush particularly abundant.

4 Saundersfoot: 1764, 2 houses; 1810, 8 houses; 1945, 30 houses. 1829, harbour started; 11,500 tons anthracite exported (1833); 38,600 tons (1864). Railway arrives (1866); last shipload exported (1930).

5 Two horizontal mine shafts (adits).

6 Path here is along the colliery tramway that connected Stepaside to Saundersfoot.

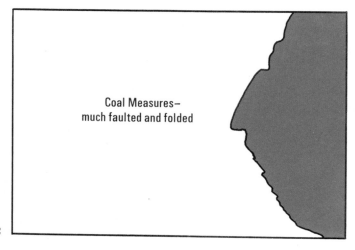

Coal Measures—
much faulted and folded

1 Coal exported from this beach around 1800.

2 See 12, p. 112.

3 Blue clay, with stumps of trees visible at exceptional spring low tides—the "drowned forest" *c.* 5000 B.C. (cf. breaking Dover–Calais landbridge).

4 Eighteenth-century house on Norman site.

1 Male Fern. 2 Lady Fern. 3 Common Polypody. 4 Hart's-tongue. 5 Sear Spleenwort.

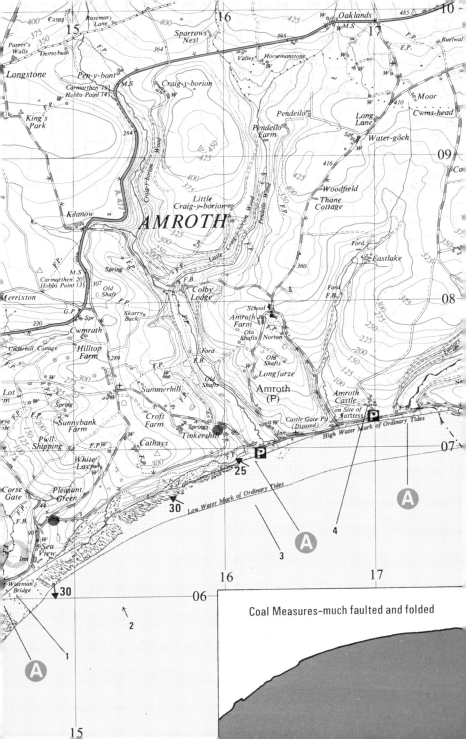

Coal Measures—much faulted and folded

Facilities for walkers

Accommodation

Because the quantity and kind of accommodation changes from year to year, any list is at once out of date. An annual Register of holiday accommodation may be had from the Pembrokeshire Community Council in return for a stamped and addressed, 7 in. × 10 in., envelope.

The Wales Tourist Board, Welcome House, Llandaf, Cardiff, also issues "Where to stay in South Wales" which may be used to supplement the local list.

Bus services

Bus routes are shadowy. Details of time-tables may be had from The Western Welsh Omnibus Company Ltd., Cambrian Yard, Haverfordwest (Tel. Haverfordwest 3284), or Manchester Square, Milford Haven (Milford 3172). W. L. Silcox and Son, 17 Water St., Pembroke Dock (Pembroke 3143), cover the area south of the Haven. The Haverfordwest–St. David's route is run by H. Collins, Cuffern, Roch, Haverfordwest (Camrose 337); and the Haverfordwest–Fishguard route is in the hands of Pioneer Motors, Newport (Newport 217).

In summer a special Coast Path bus service runs, linking all the coastal car parks from Dale to Newgale, so that walkers are no longer hampered by having to return to their cars. Timetables are available from all National Park Information Centres.

Comments and complaints

Paradoxically, the more the path is used the easier it will be to maintain. In the ordinary course of events stiles may get broken, landslides carry a yard or two of path into the sea, lengths of the path may become overgrown or impassably boggy, waymarking may not be adequate. Notifications of such deficiencies are gratefully received by The National Park Warden (Long-Distance Path), County Council Offices, Haverfordwest, Pembrokeshire. Users of the path are asked not to be reticent with their suggestions for improving the amenities of the path.

Book list

Space restricts me to listing only a few of the references likely
to be useful to those walking the path. A fuller bibliography
is in the *Pembrokeshire Coast National Park Guide* (HMSO).

Barrett, J. H. (1959): The Birds of the Parish of Dale, including
Skokholm. *Field Studies* 1.i. 1–16.

Bassett, D. A. and Bassett, M. G. (*eds.*) (1971): *Geological
Excursions in South Wales and the Forest of Dean.* H. J.
Lear, Cardiff.

Bowen, E. G. (1954): *The Settlements of the Celtic Saints in
Wales.* University of Wales Press, Cardiff.

Bowen, E. G. (1969): *Saints, Seaways and Settlements.* University of Wales Press, Cardiff.

Dalby, D. H. (1966): The Bryophytes of the Parish of Dale.
Field Studies 2.iii. 283–301.

Dalby, D. H. (1970): The Salt Marshes of Milford Haven,
Pembrokeshire. *Field Studies* 3.ii. 297–330.

Edwards, George (1963): The Coal Industry in Pembrokeshire.
Field Studies 1.v. 33–64.

Ferry, B. W. (1971): The Lichens of the Dale Peninsula and
other nearby Localities. *Field Studies* 3.iii. 481–496.

George, Barbara (1964): Pembrokeshire Sea-Trading before
1900. *Field Studies* 2.i. 1–39.

George, Martin (1961): The flowering Plants and Ferns of
Dale, Pembrokeshire. *Field Studies* 1.iii. 21–44.

Gilpin, M. C. (1960): Population Changes round the Shores of
Milford Haven from 1800 to the present Day. *Field Studies*
1.ii. 23–36.

John, Brian (1972): *The Fishguard and Pembrokeshire Area.*
British Landscapes through Maps, No. 16. Geog. Association.

John, Brian and Evans, Robert (1973): *The Pembrokeshire
Landscape.* Five Arches Press, Tenby.

Jones, E. H. Stuart (1950): *The last Invasion of Britain.* University of Wales Press, Cardiff.

Jones, W. E. and Williams, R. (1966): The Seaweeds of Dale.
Field Studies 2.iii. 303–330.

Leatham, Diana (1952): *The Story of St. David of Wales*. Garraway (Wales), London.

Miles, Dillwyn (ed.) (1973): *Pembrokeshire Coast National Park Guide, No. 10.* HMSO.

Moore, Donald (*ed.*) (1970): *The Irish Sea Province in Archaeology and History*. Cardiff.

North, F. J. (1955): *The Evolution of the Bristol Channel.* Cambrian Archaeological Association, Cardiff.

Oliver, J. (1959): The Climate of the Dale Peninsula, Pembrokeshire. *Field Studies* 1.i. 40–56.

Pringle, J. and George, T. Neville (1948): *British Regional Geology: South Wales.* HMSO.

Stratton, L. W. (1964): The non-marine Mollusca of the Parish of Dale. *Field Studies* 2.i. 41–52.

Warren Davies, T. A. (1970): *Plants of Pembrokeshire*. West Wales National Trust, Haverfordwest.

The Country Code

Guard against all risk of fire

Fasten all gates

Keep dogs under proper control

Keep to the paths across farm land

Avoid damaging fences, hedges and walls

Leave no litter

Safeguard water supplies

Protect wild life, wild plants and trees

Go carefully on country roads

Respect the life of the countryside

1 Black-headed Gull. 2 Kittiwake. 3 Herring Gull. 4 Lesser Black-backed Gull (all in summer dress; also head of Black-headed Gull in winter).